Coloring with Jasmine

The Art of Coloring

Adult Coloring Book

This book is dedicated to Jasmine my great Grand daughter. Jasmine has stage 3 cancer. Royalties from this books goes into a Trust Fund for Jasmine. Thank You for Buying this book.

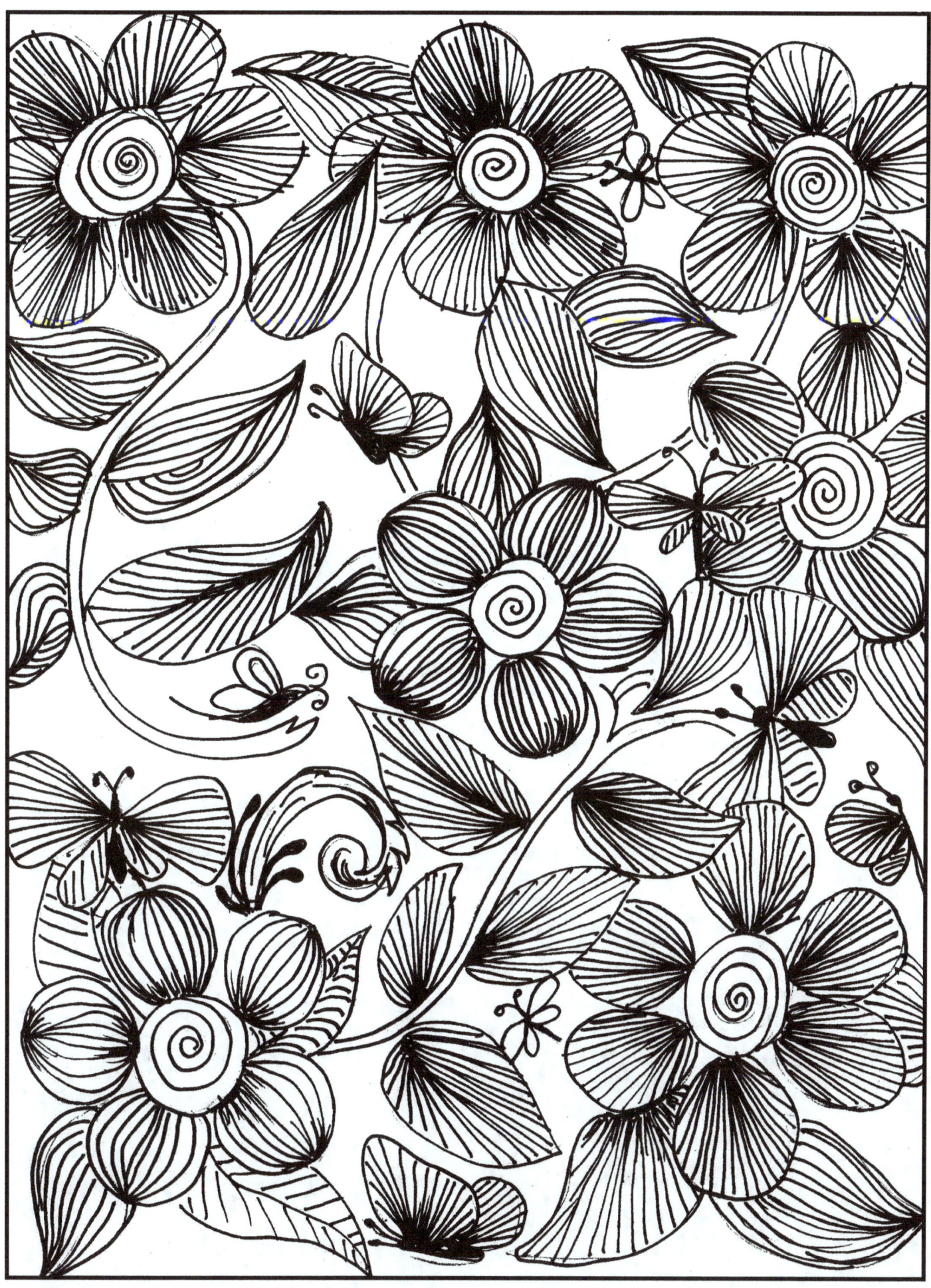

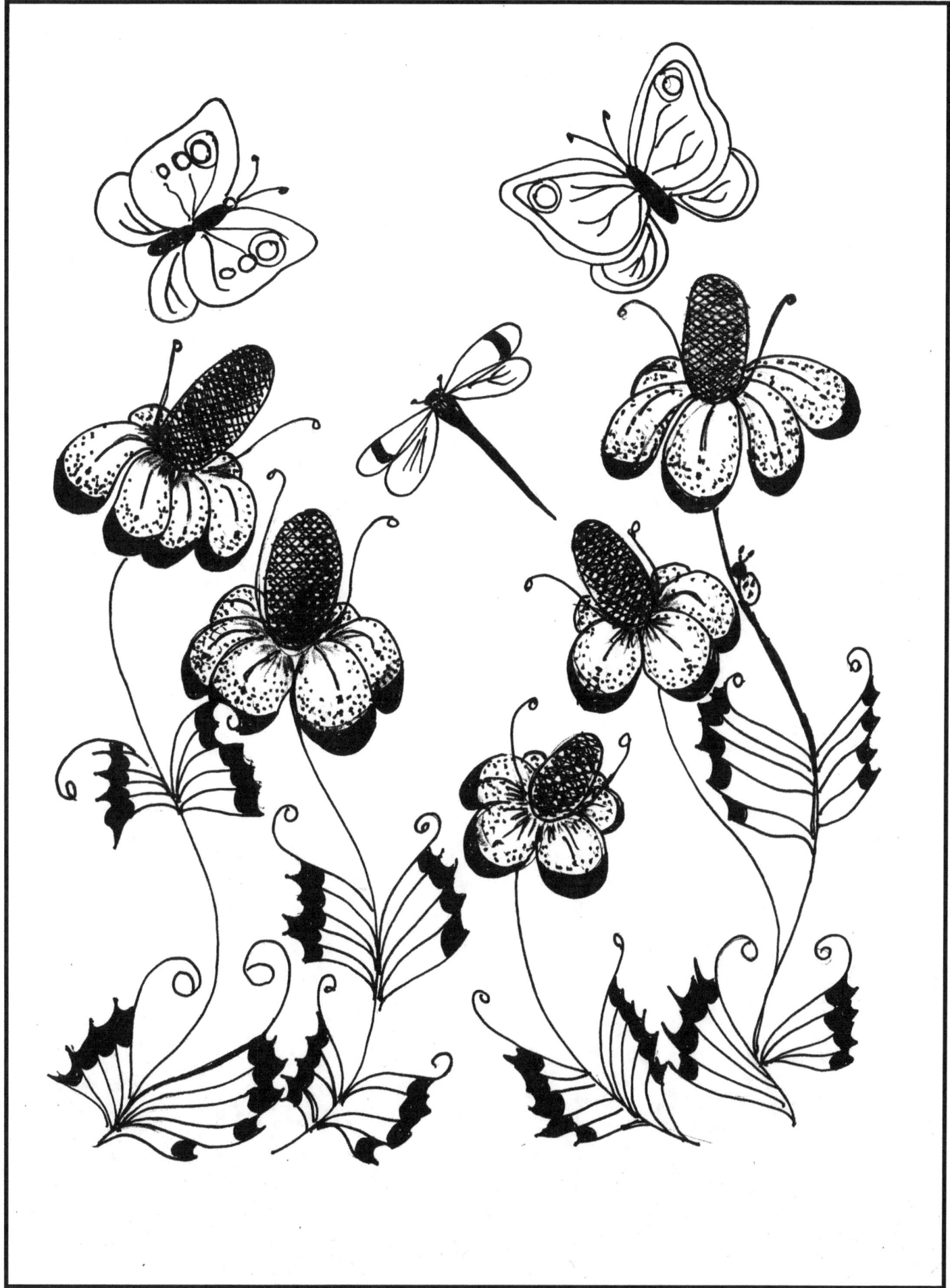

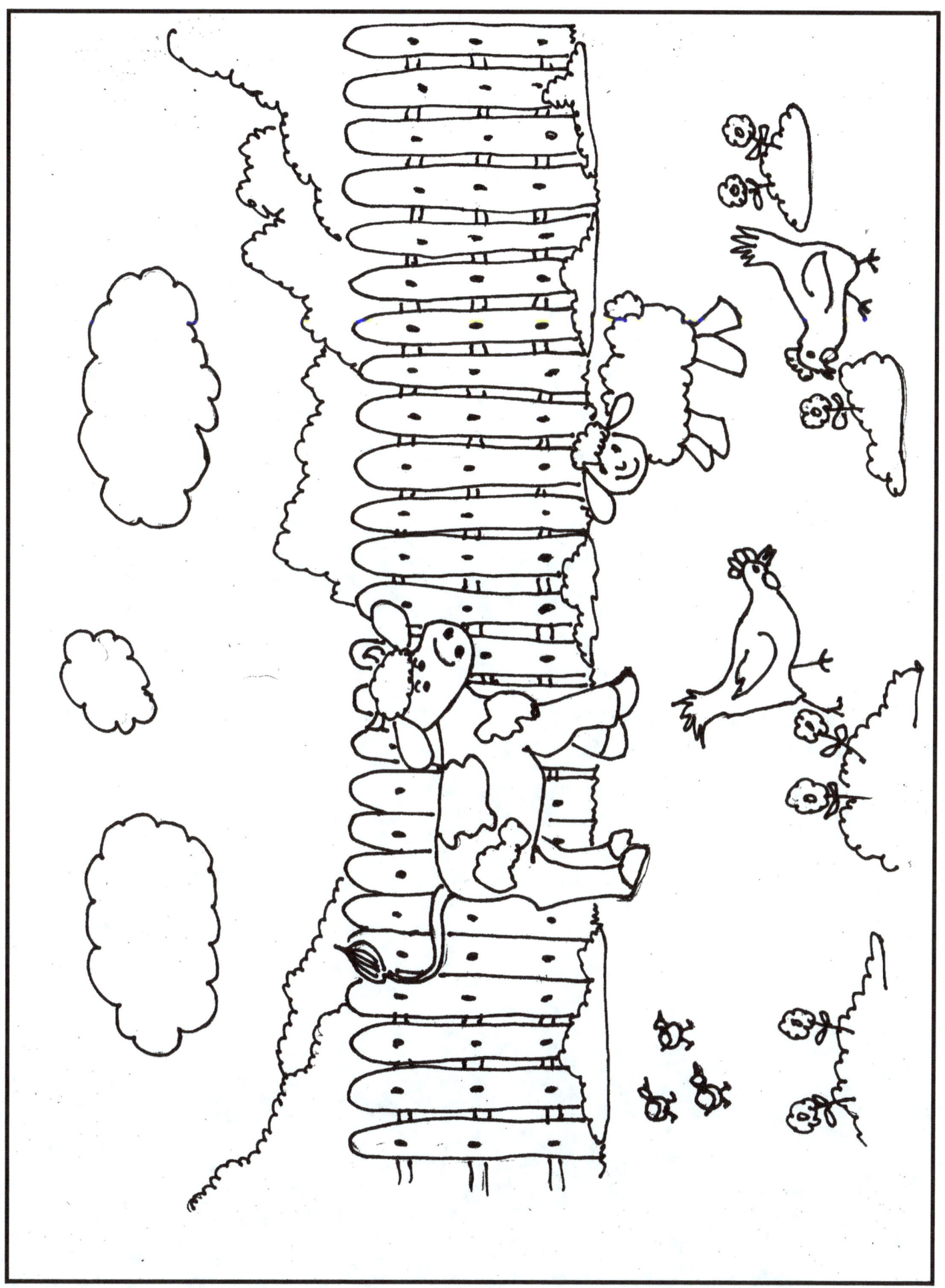

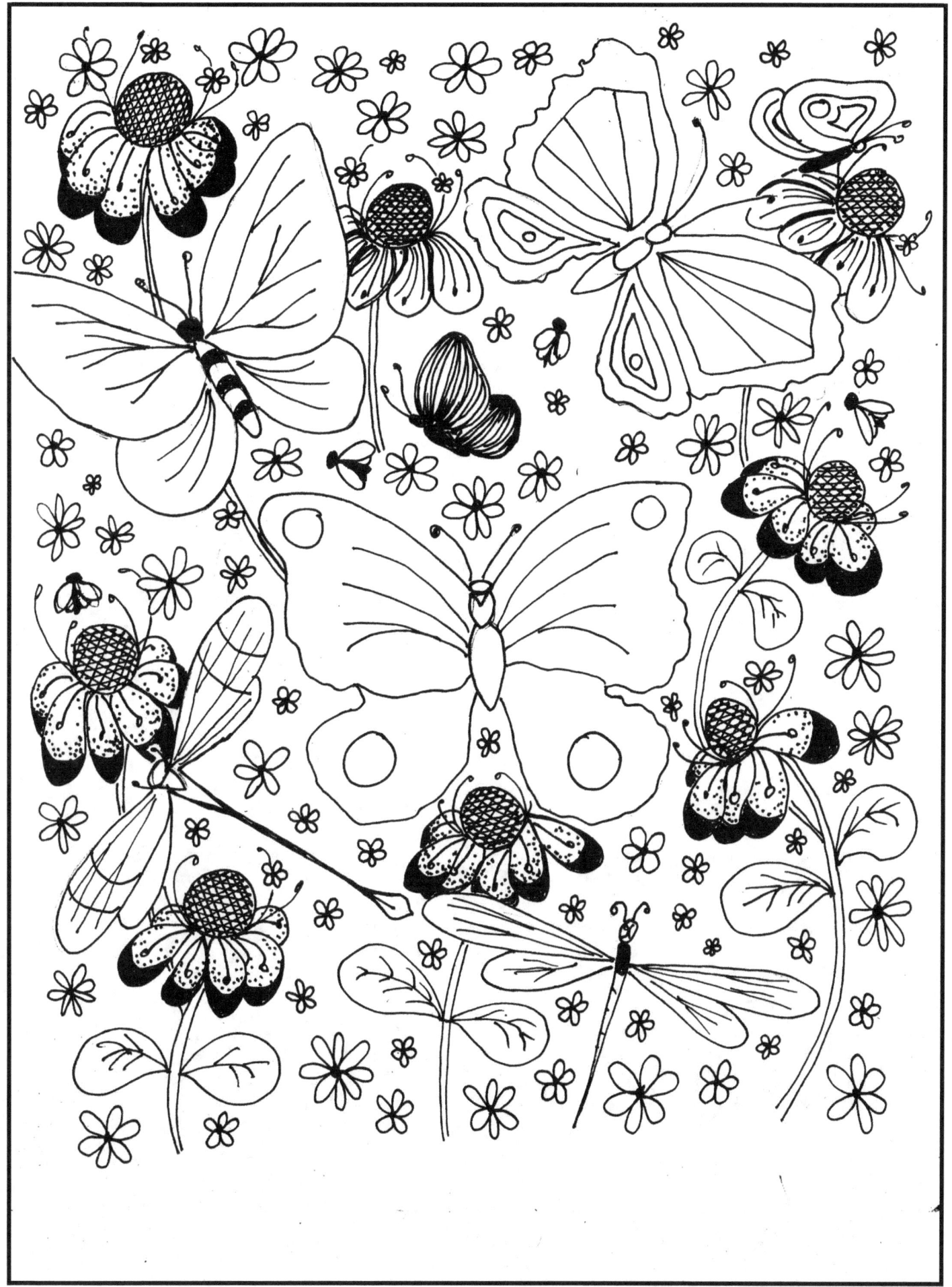

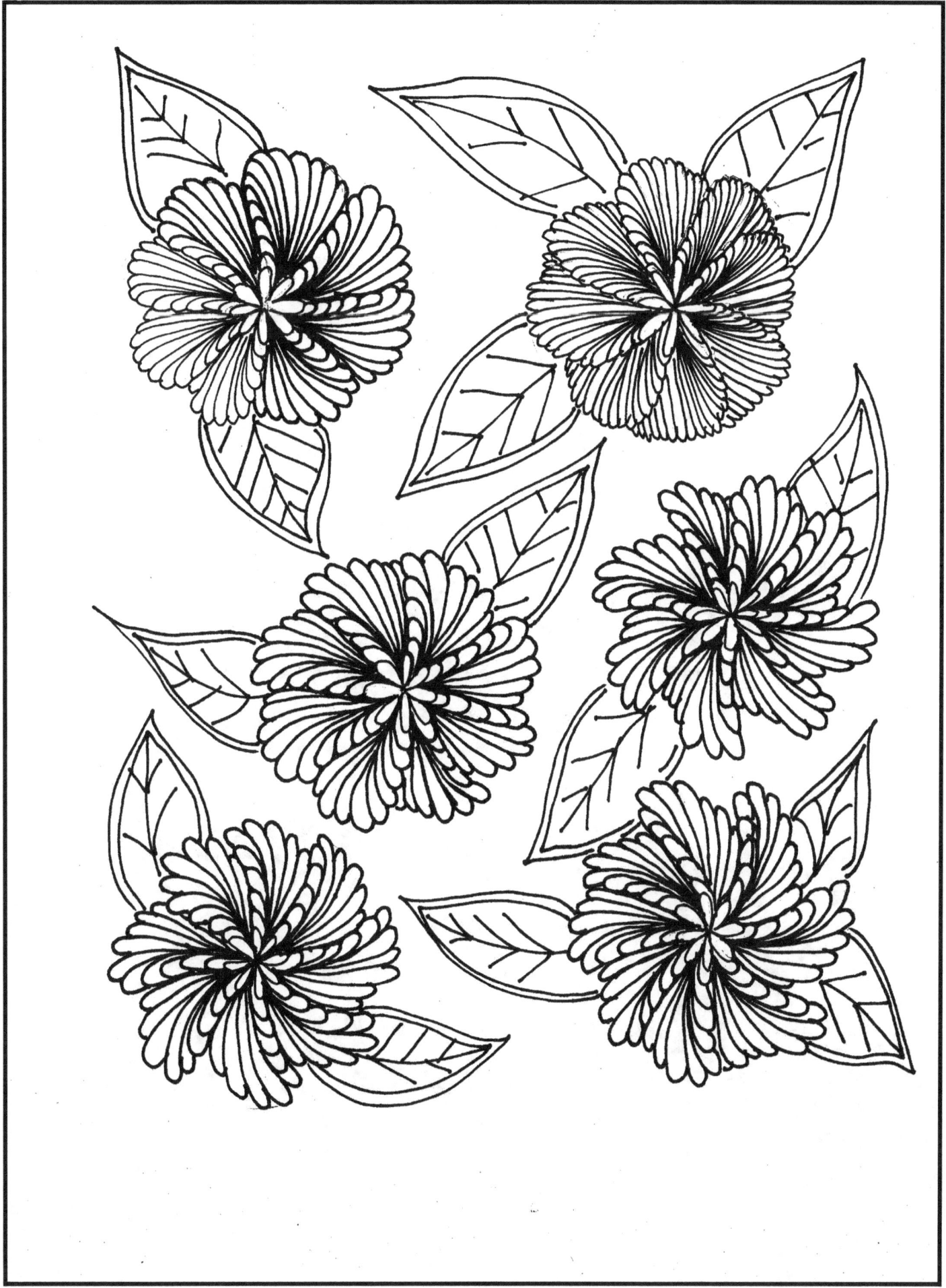

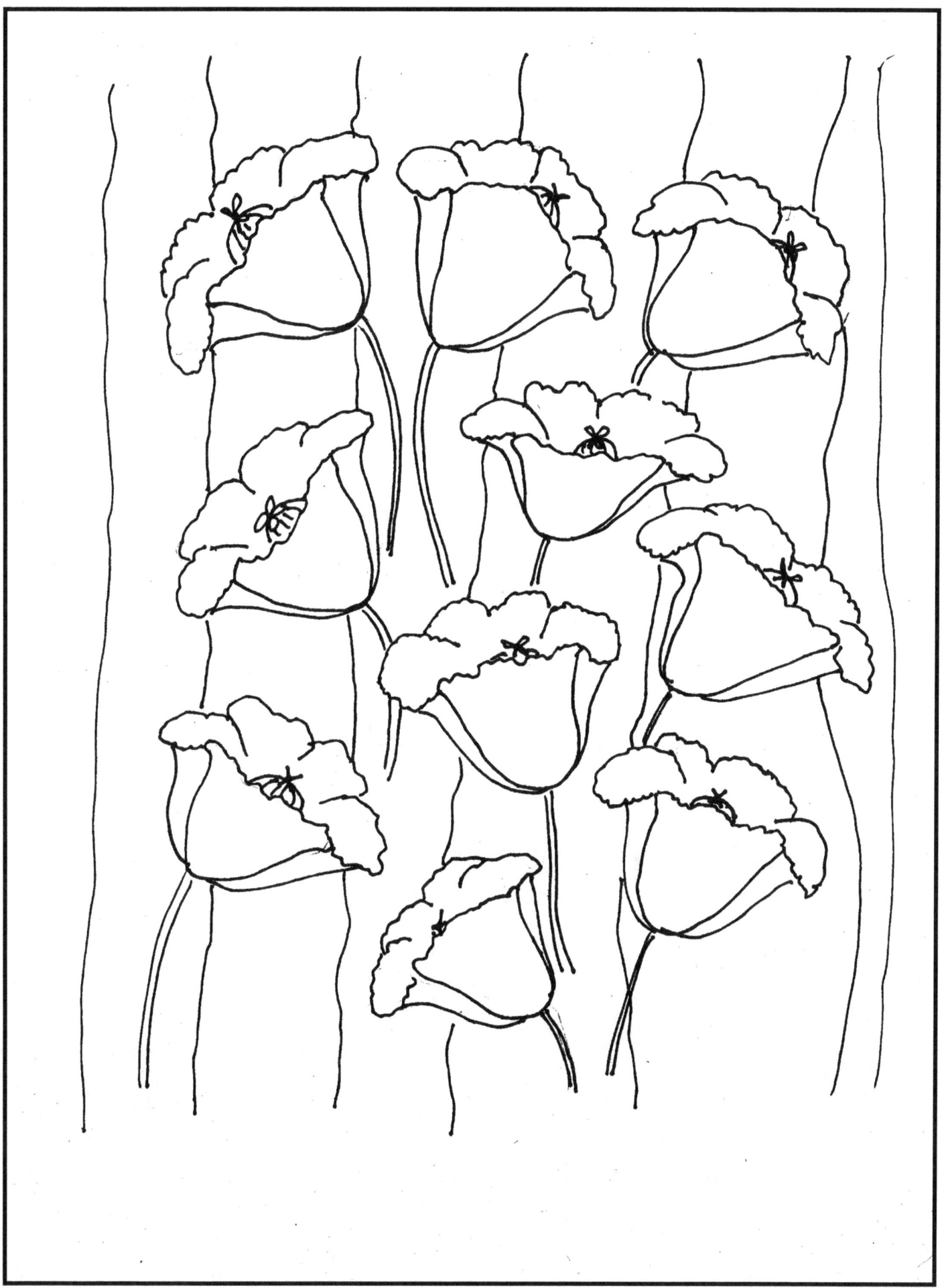

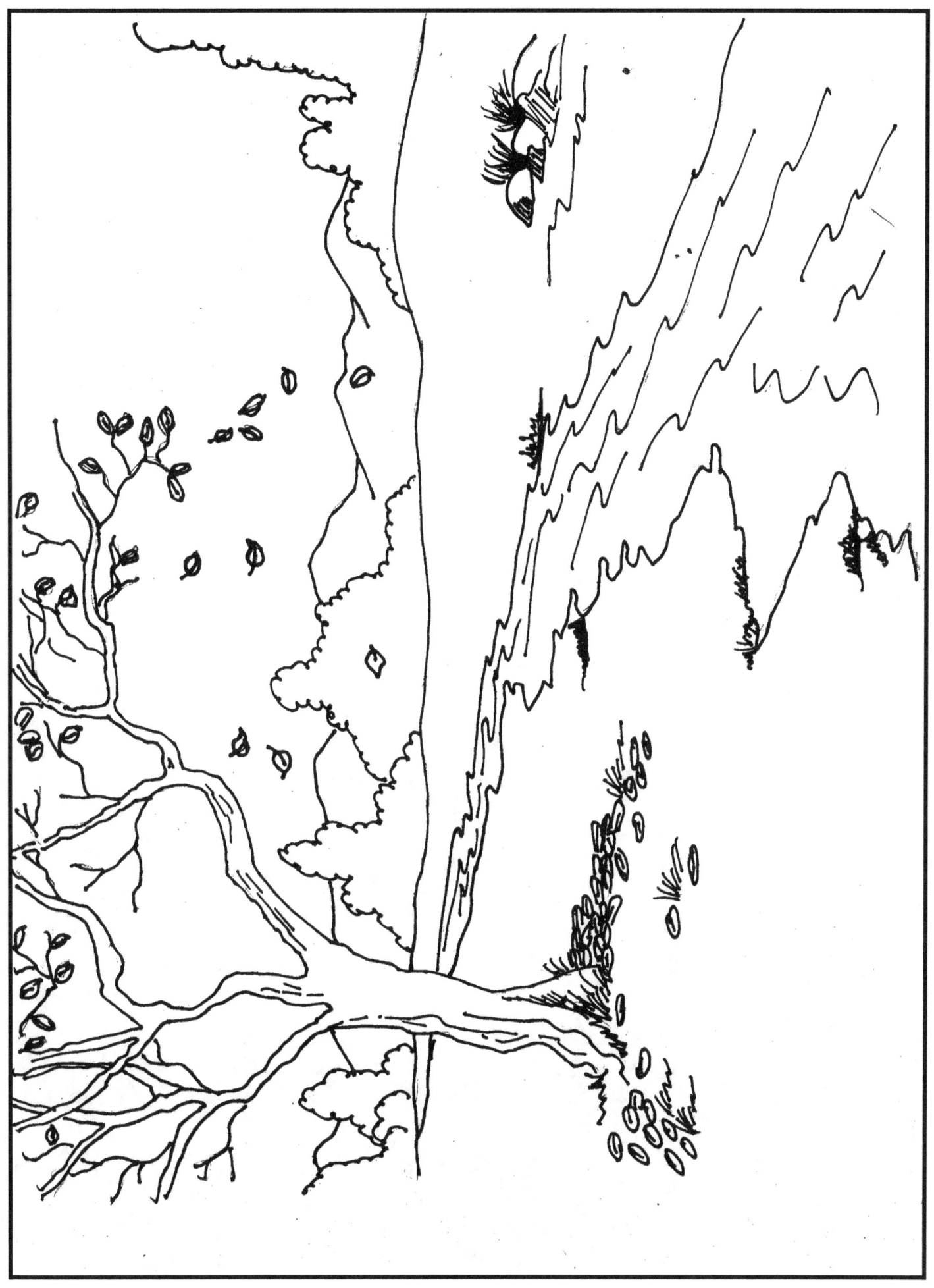

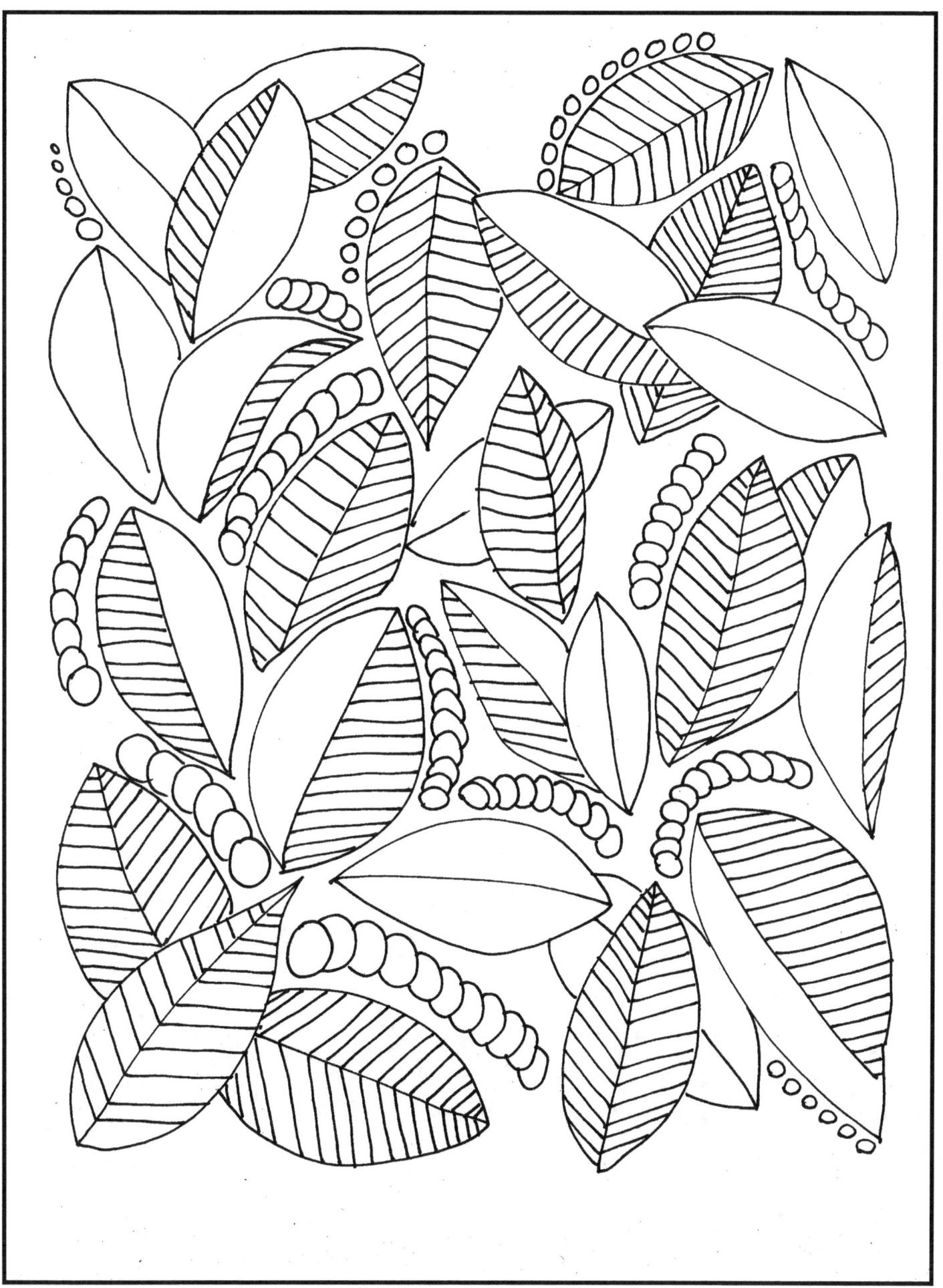

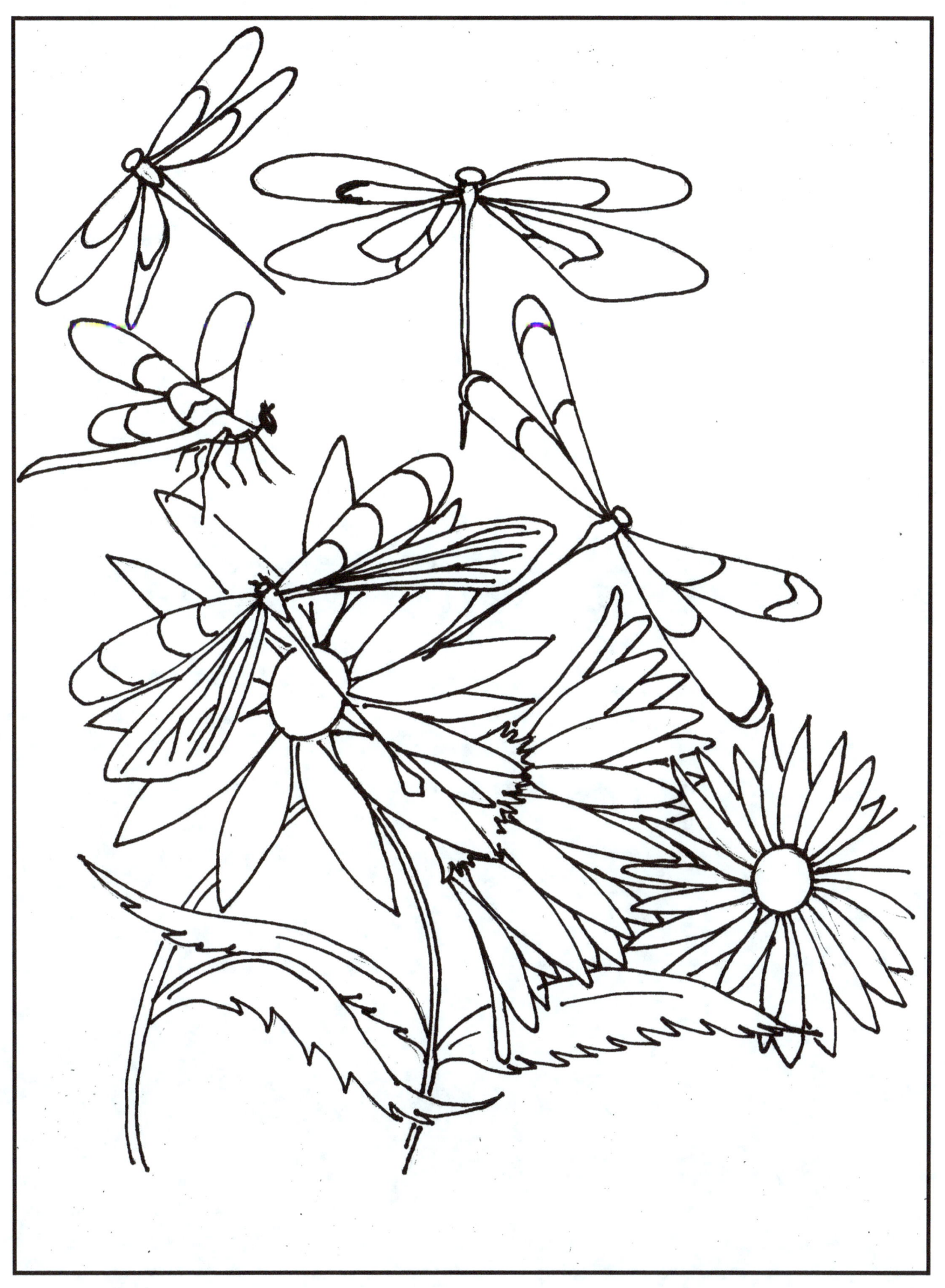

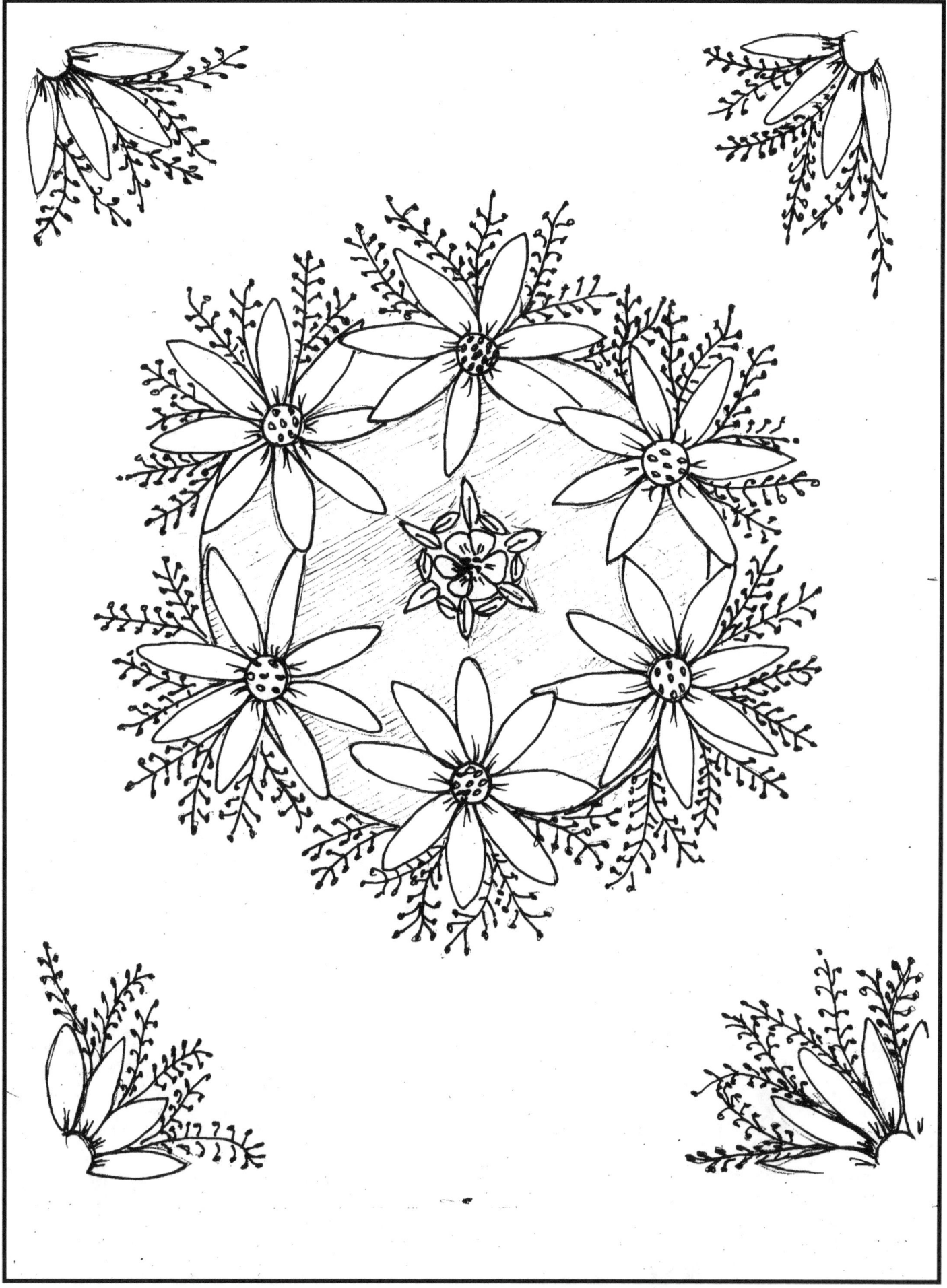

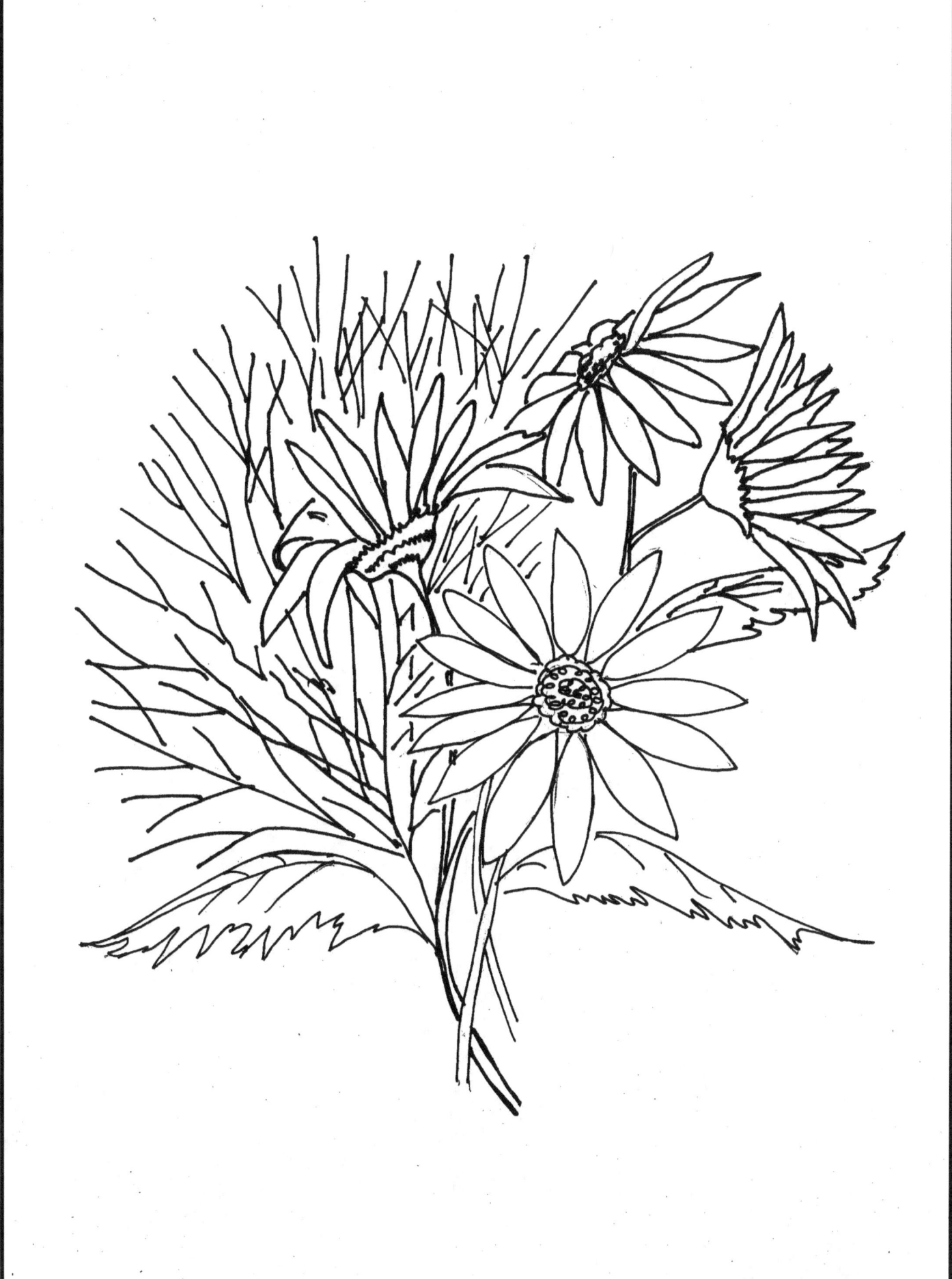

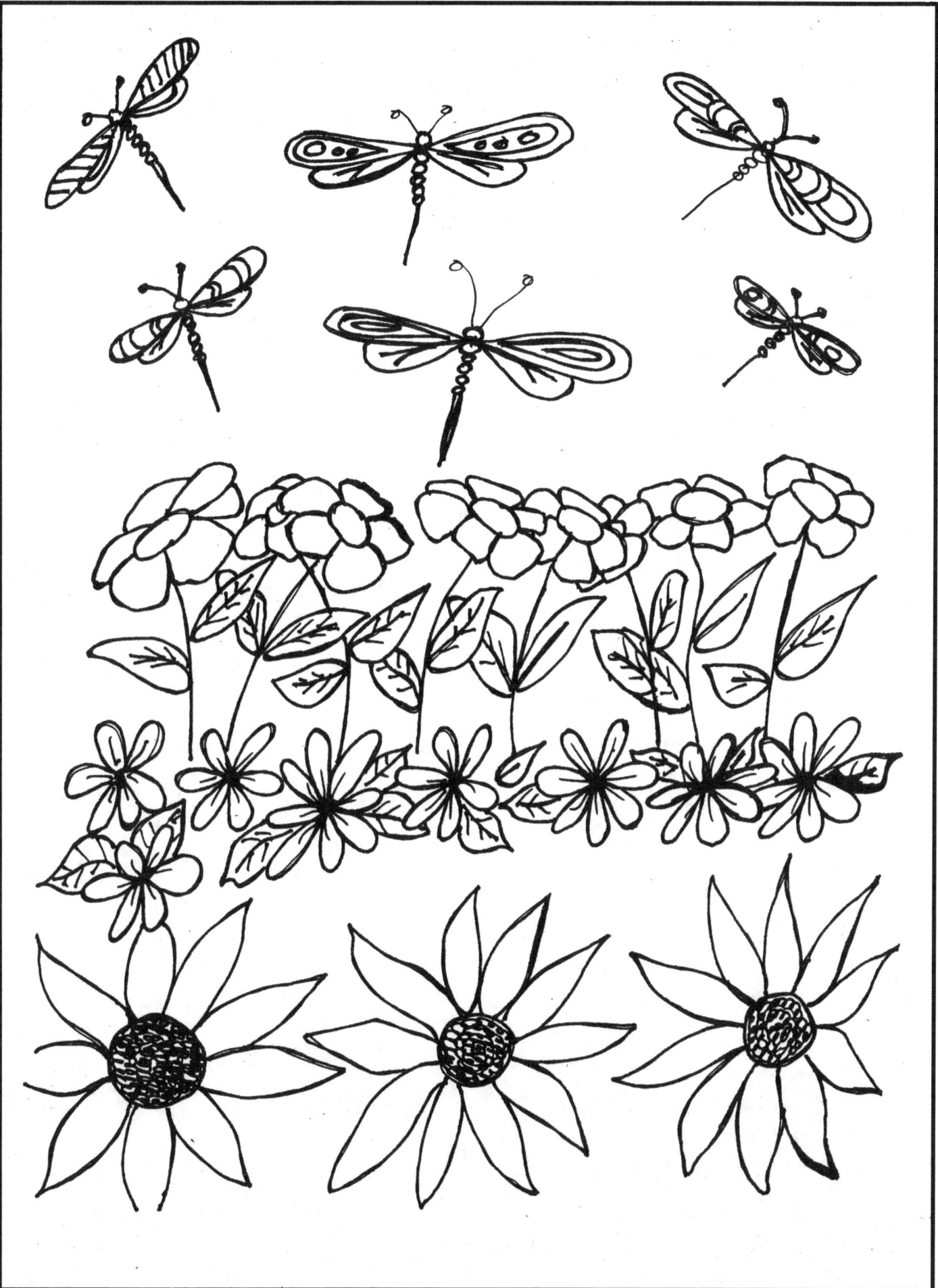

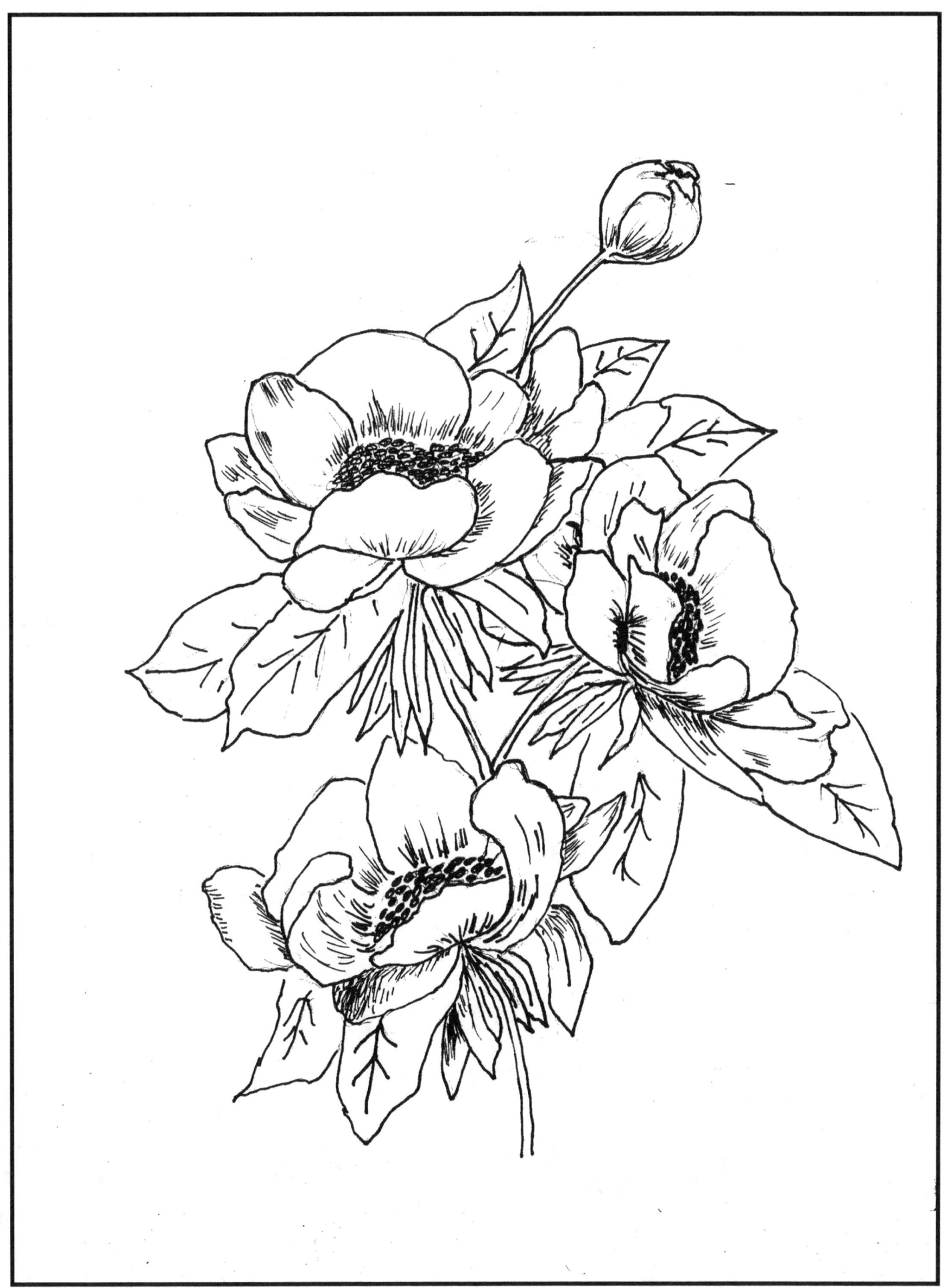

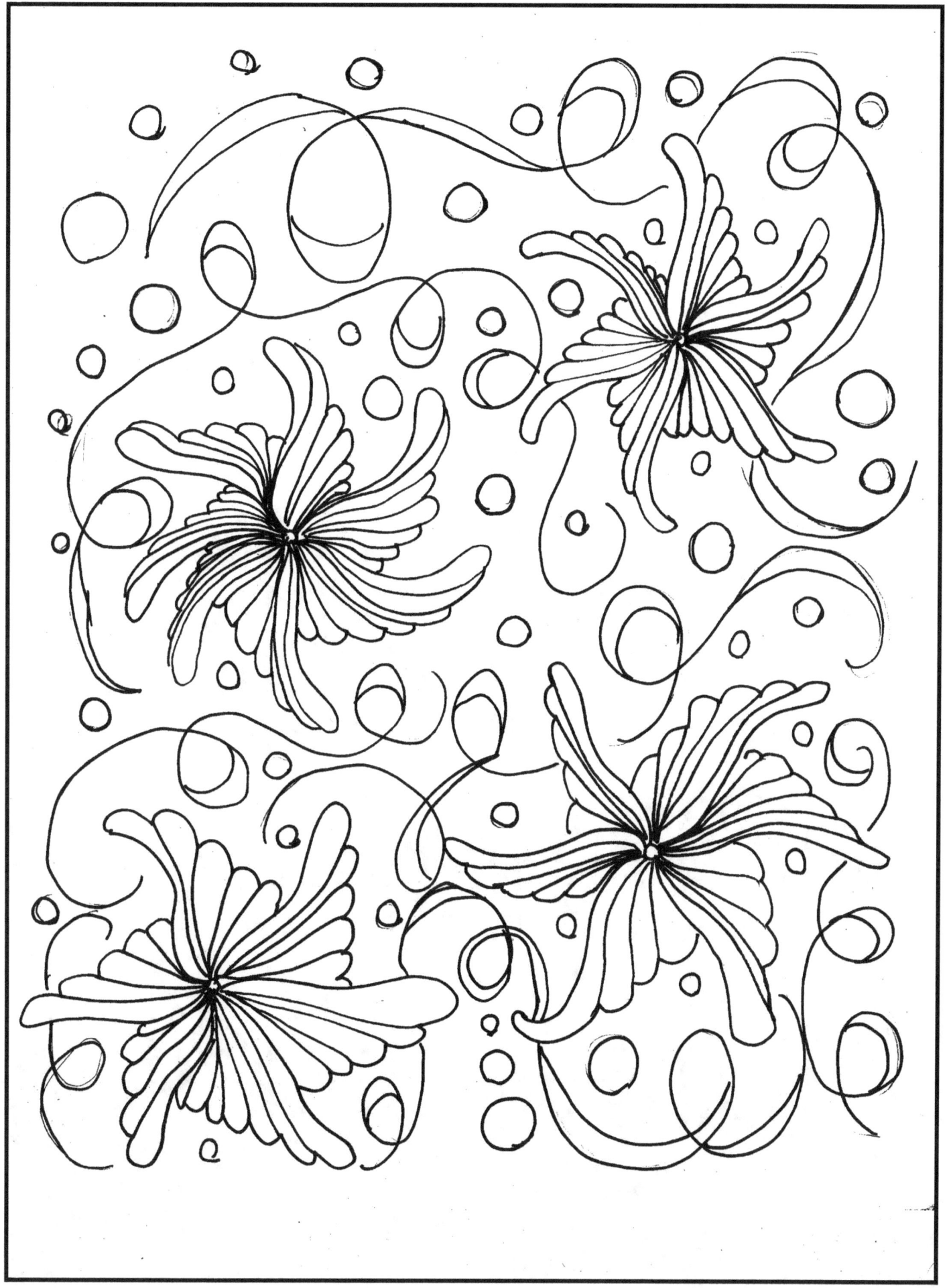

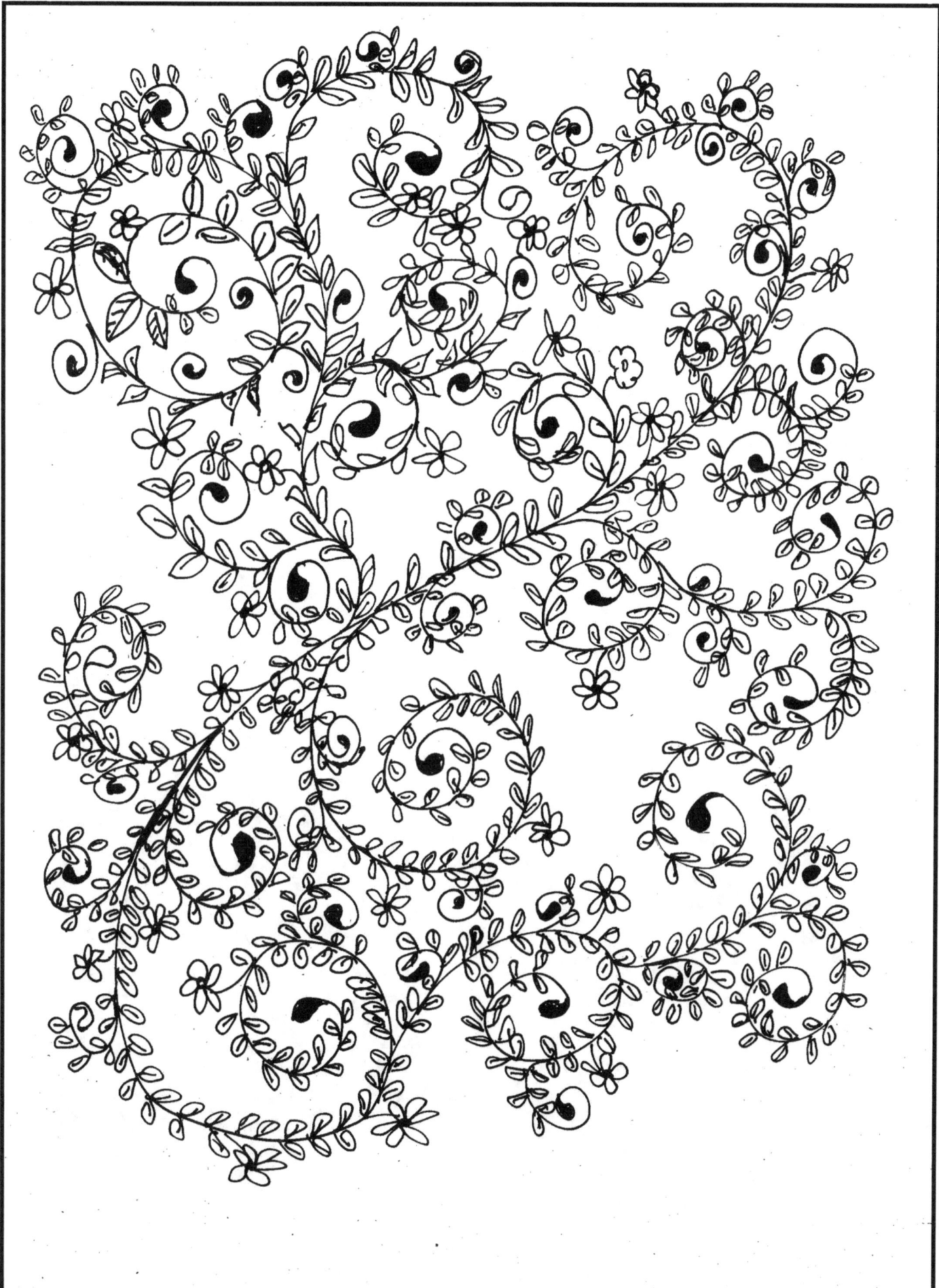

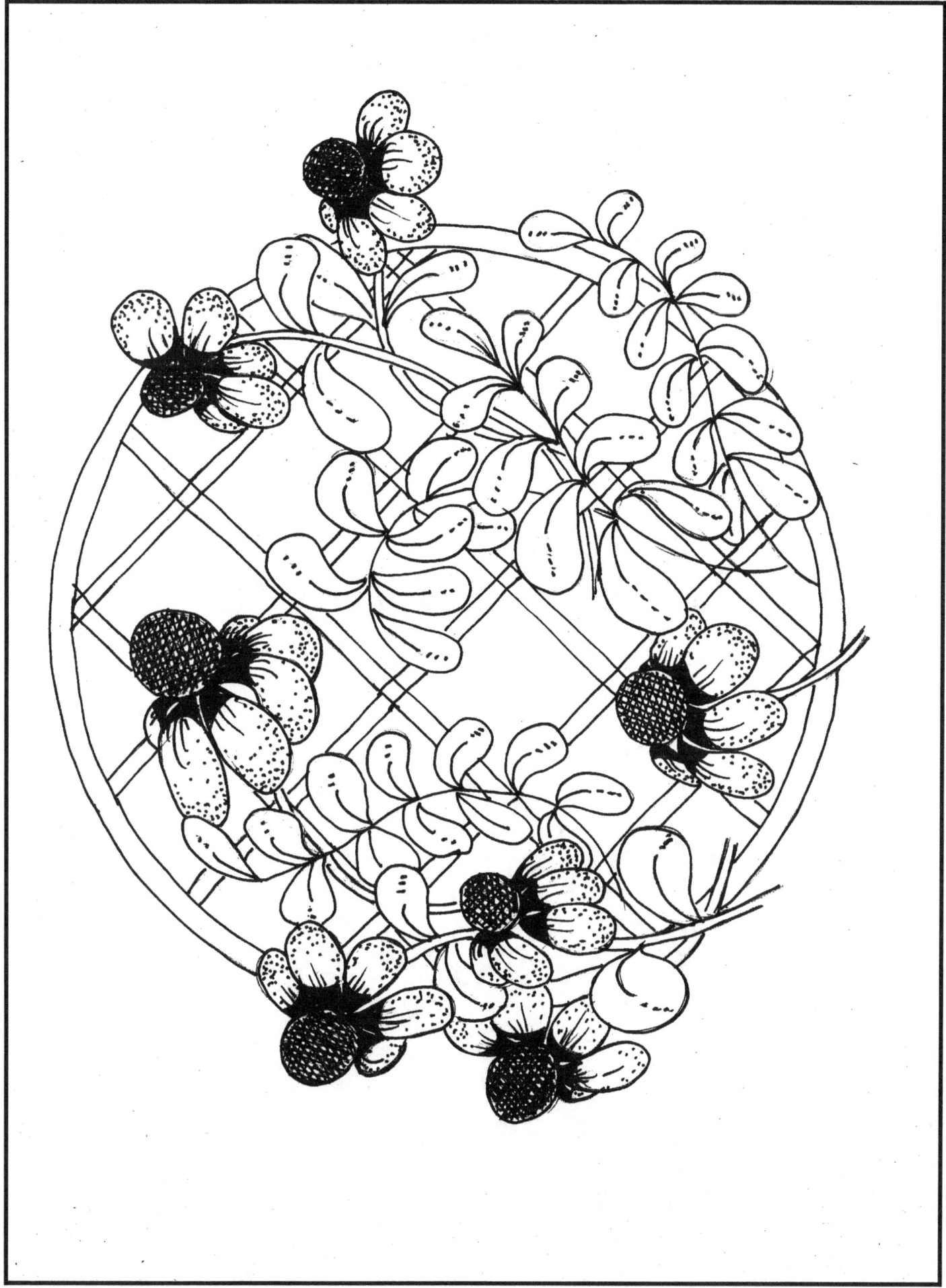

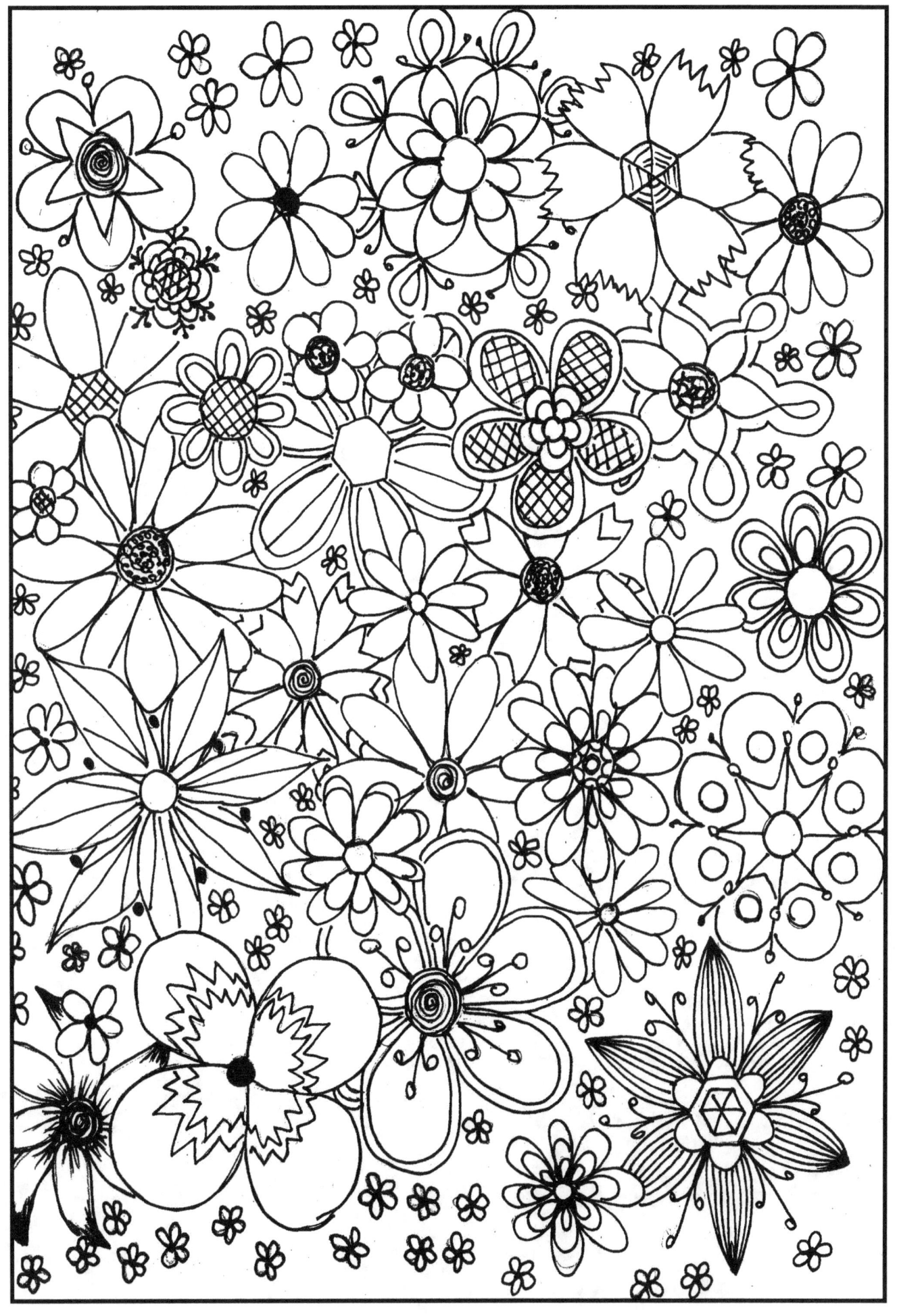

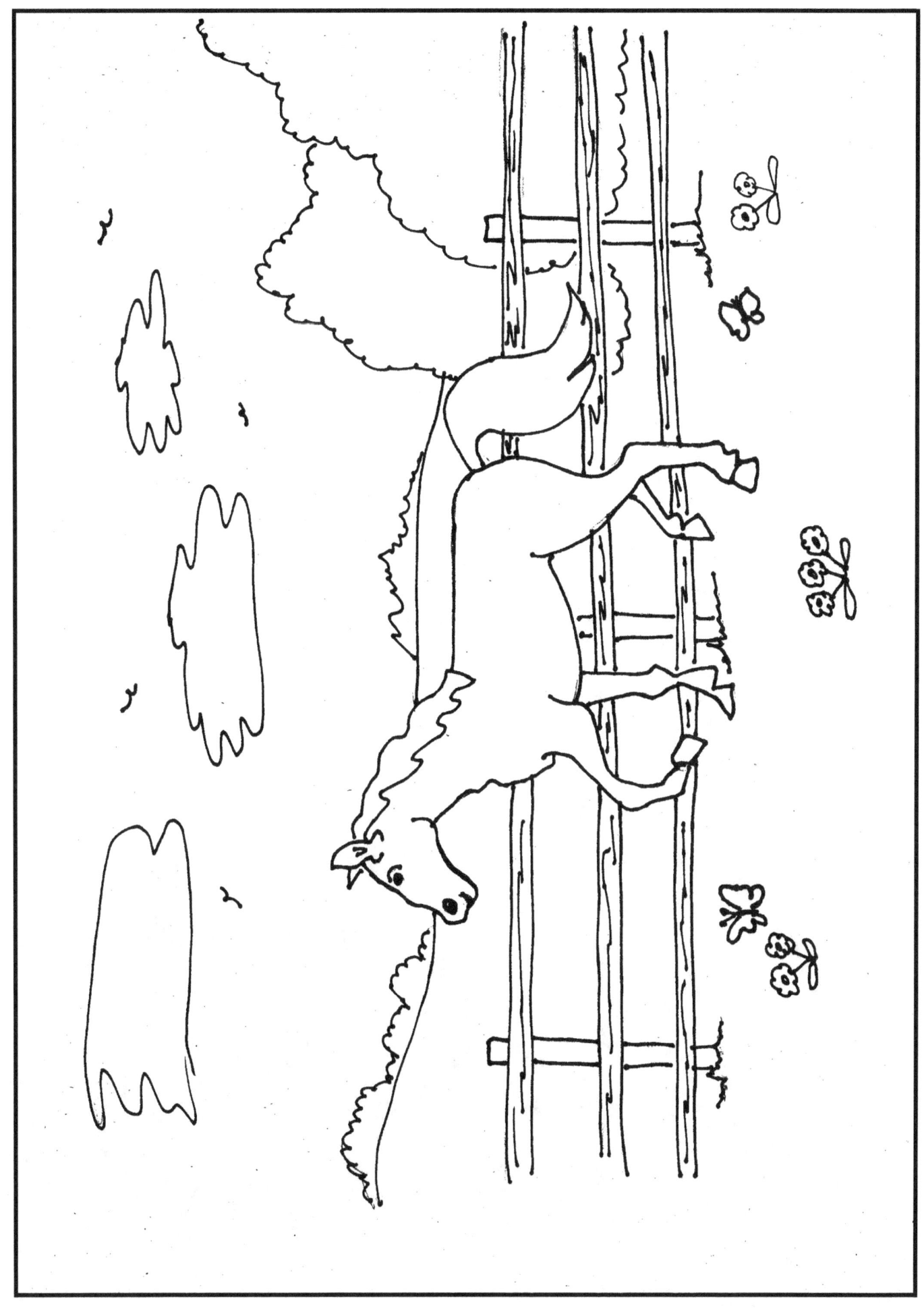

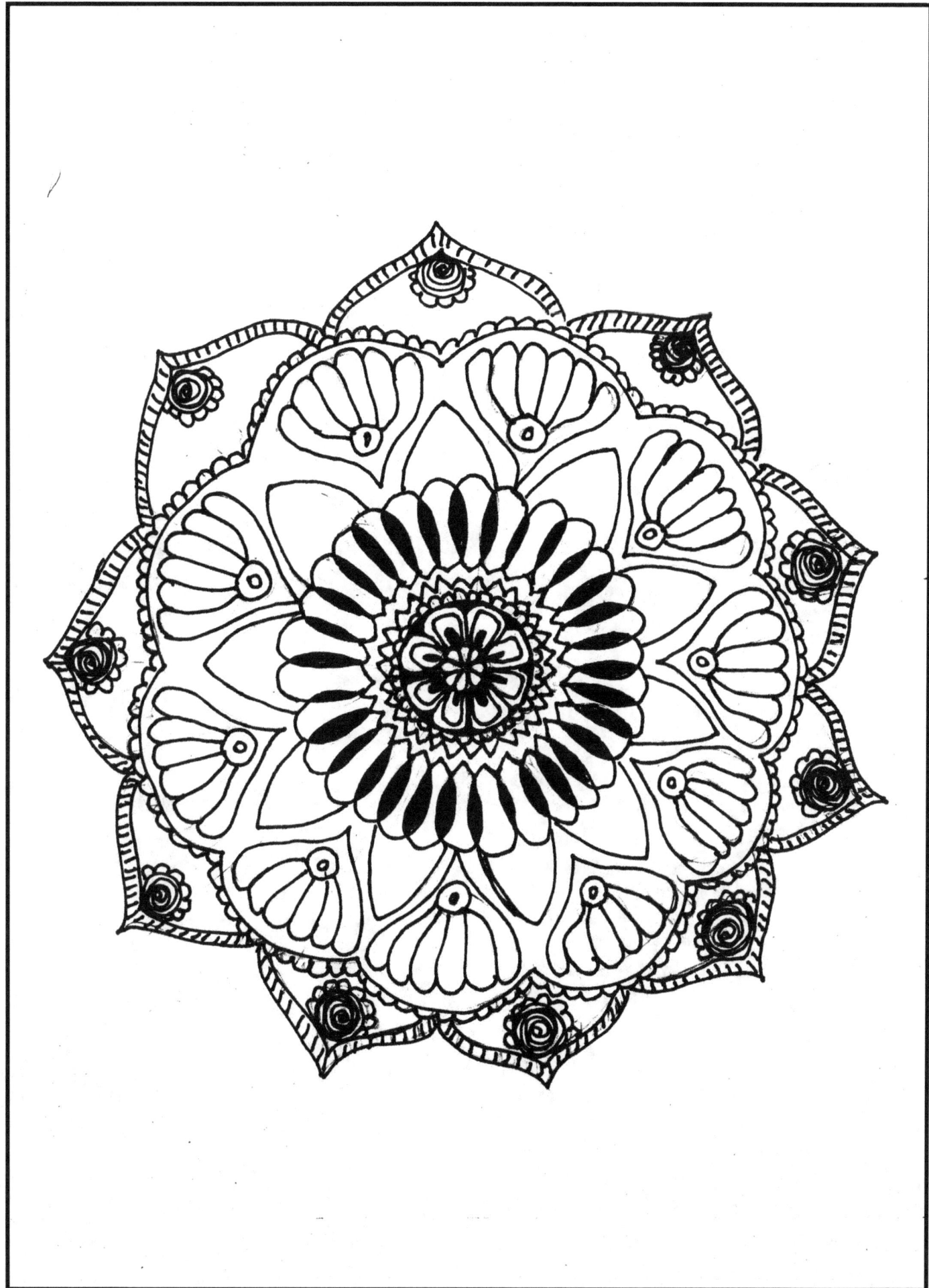

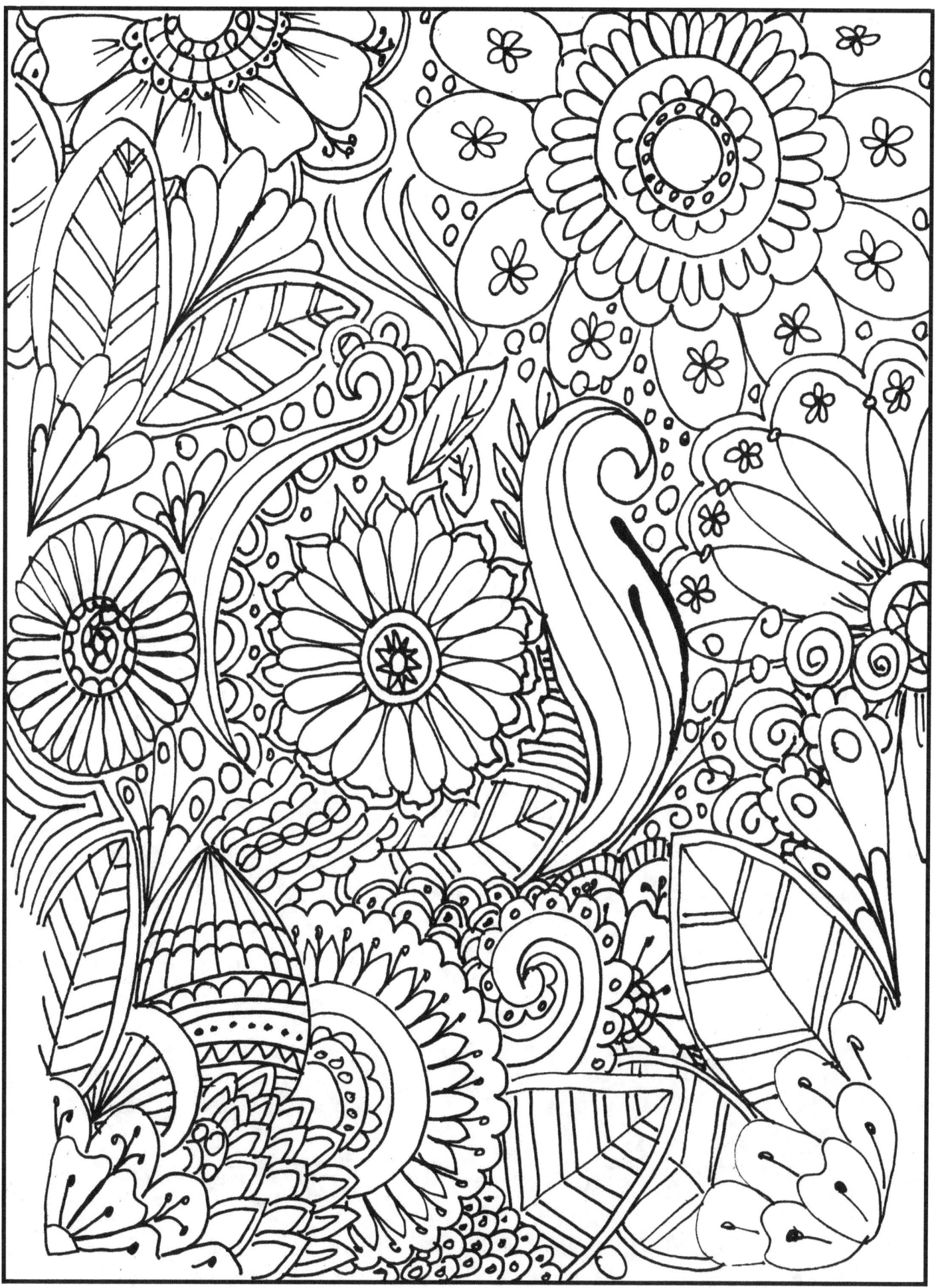

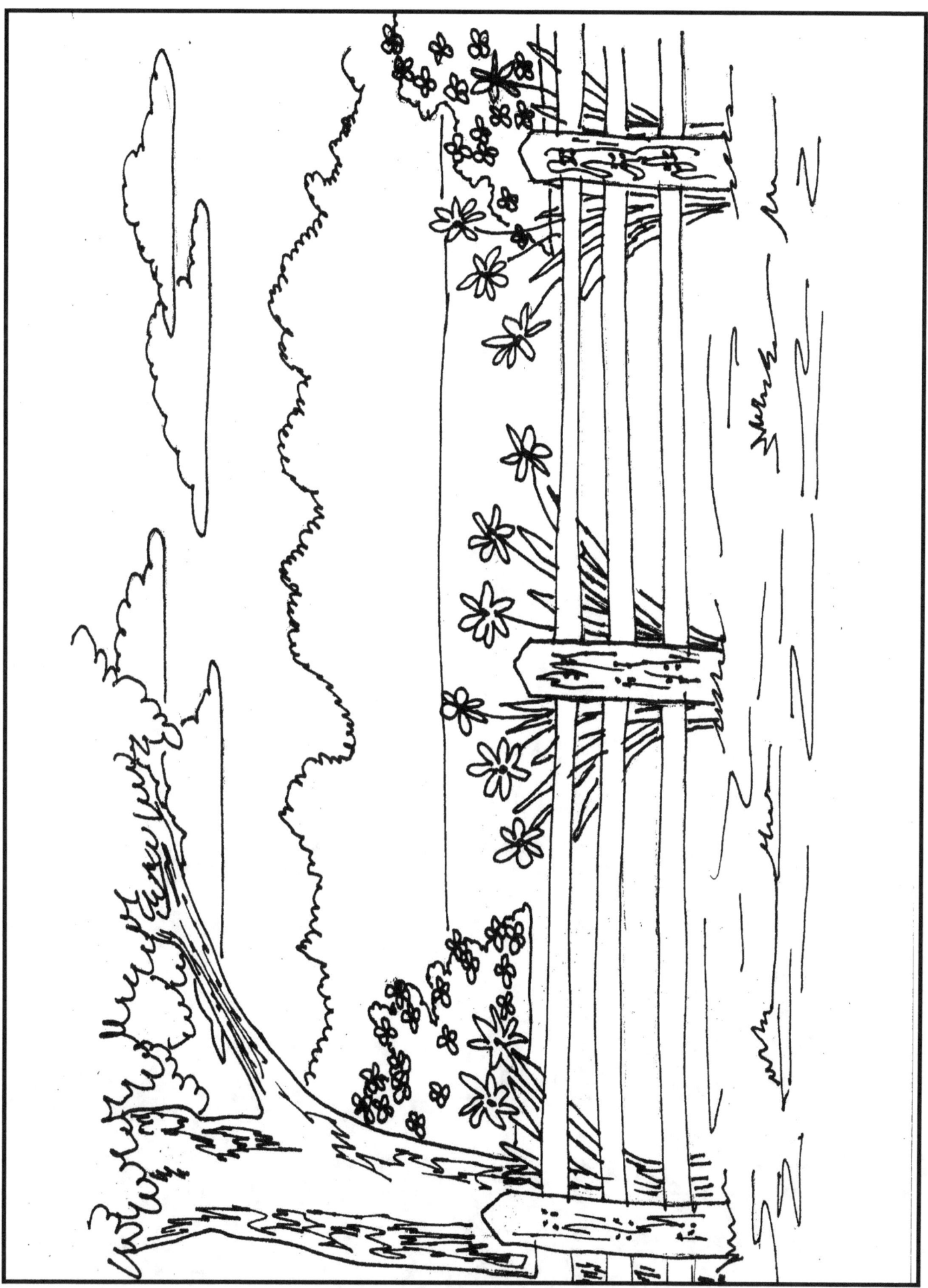

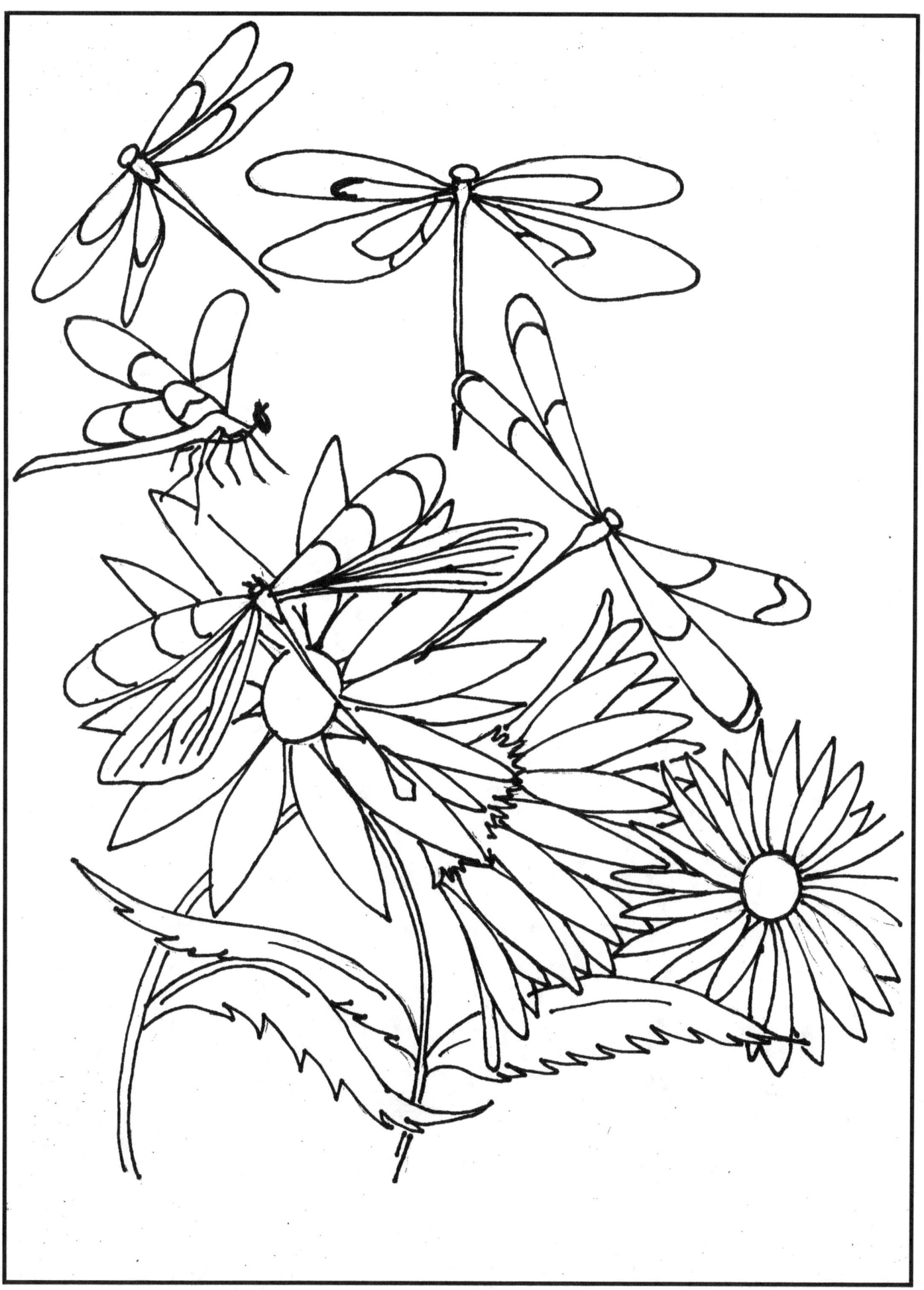

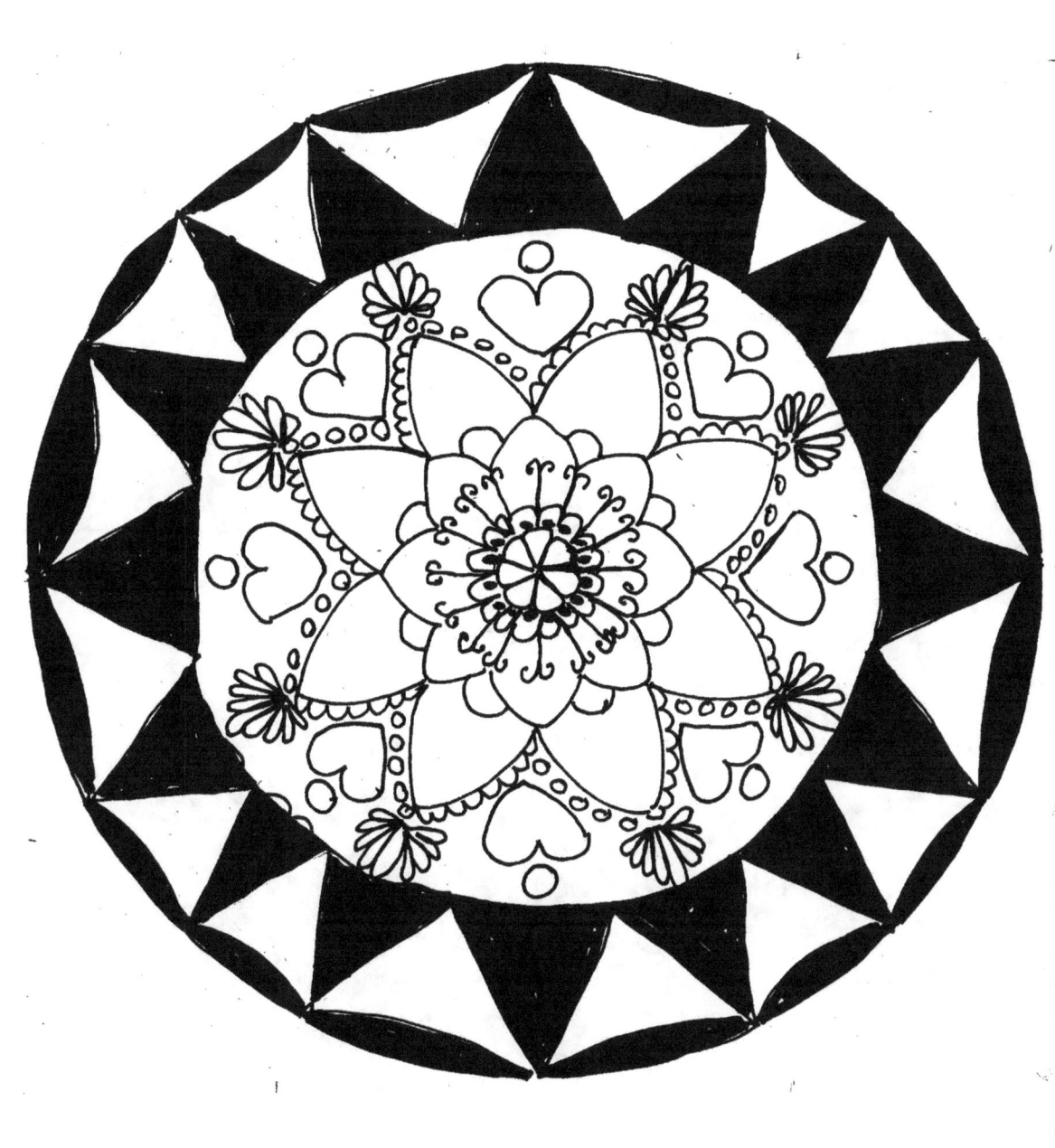

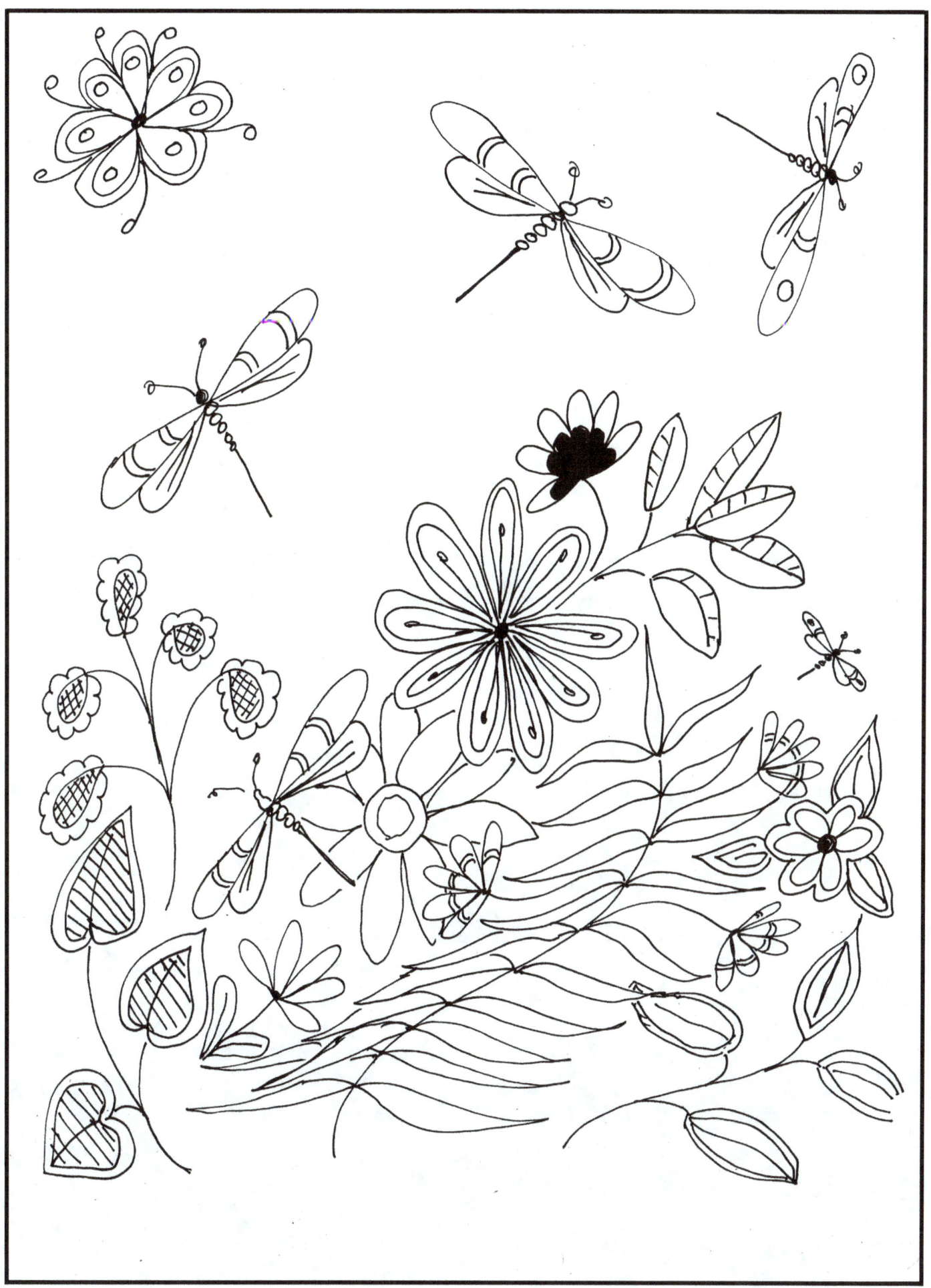

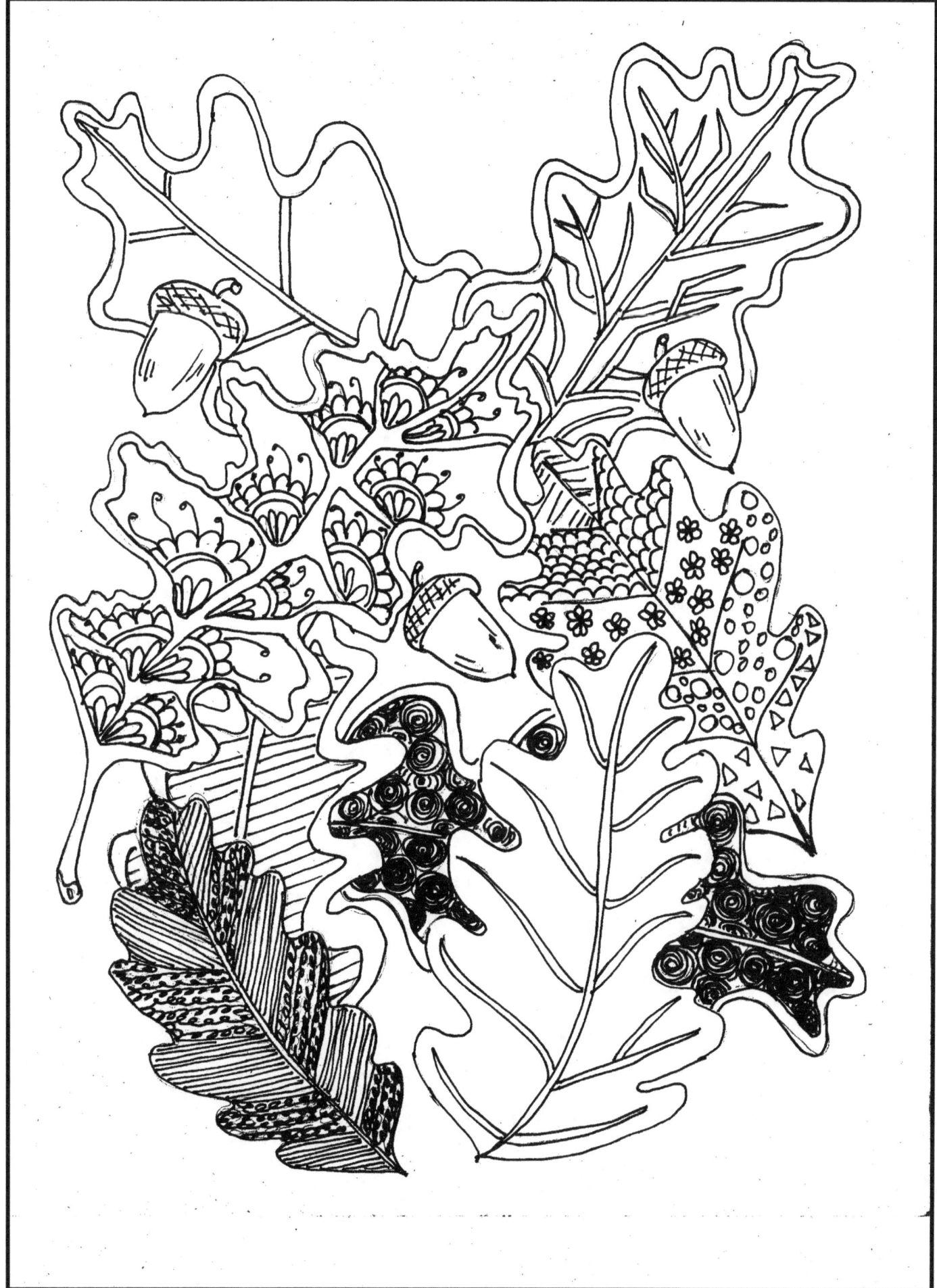

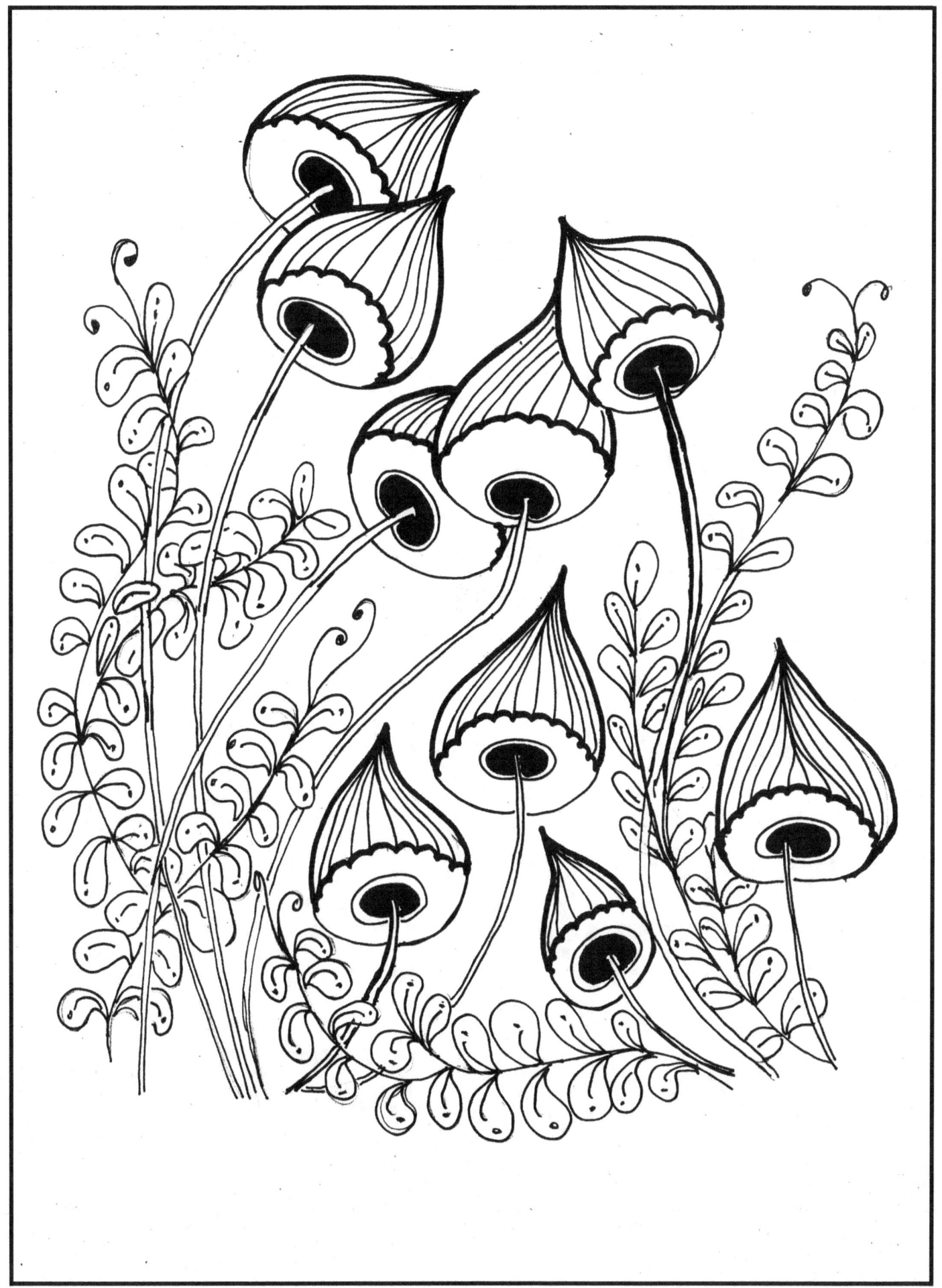

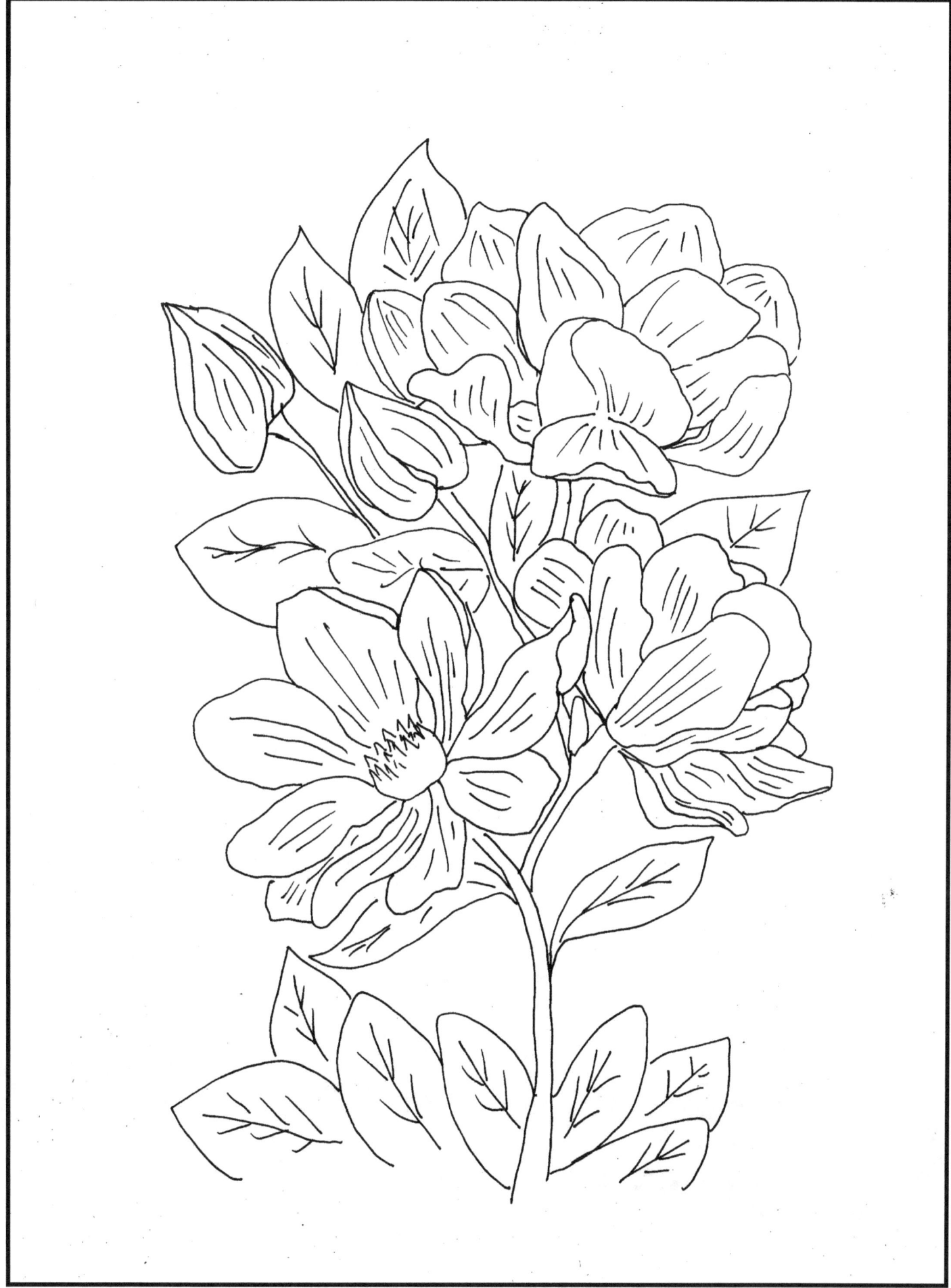

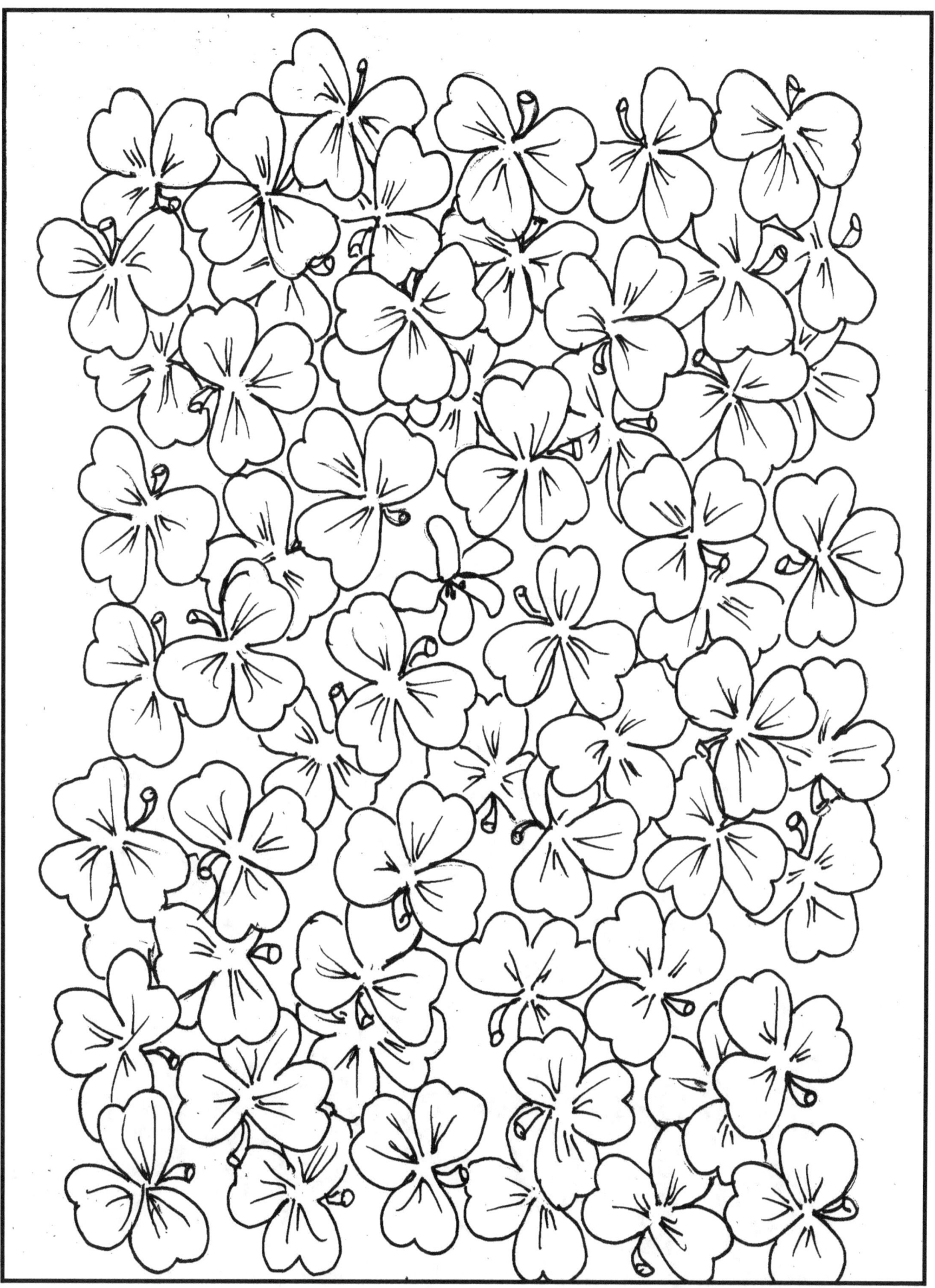

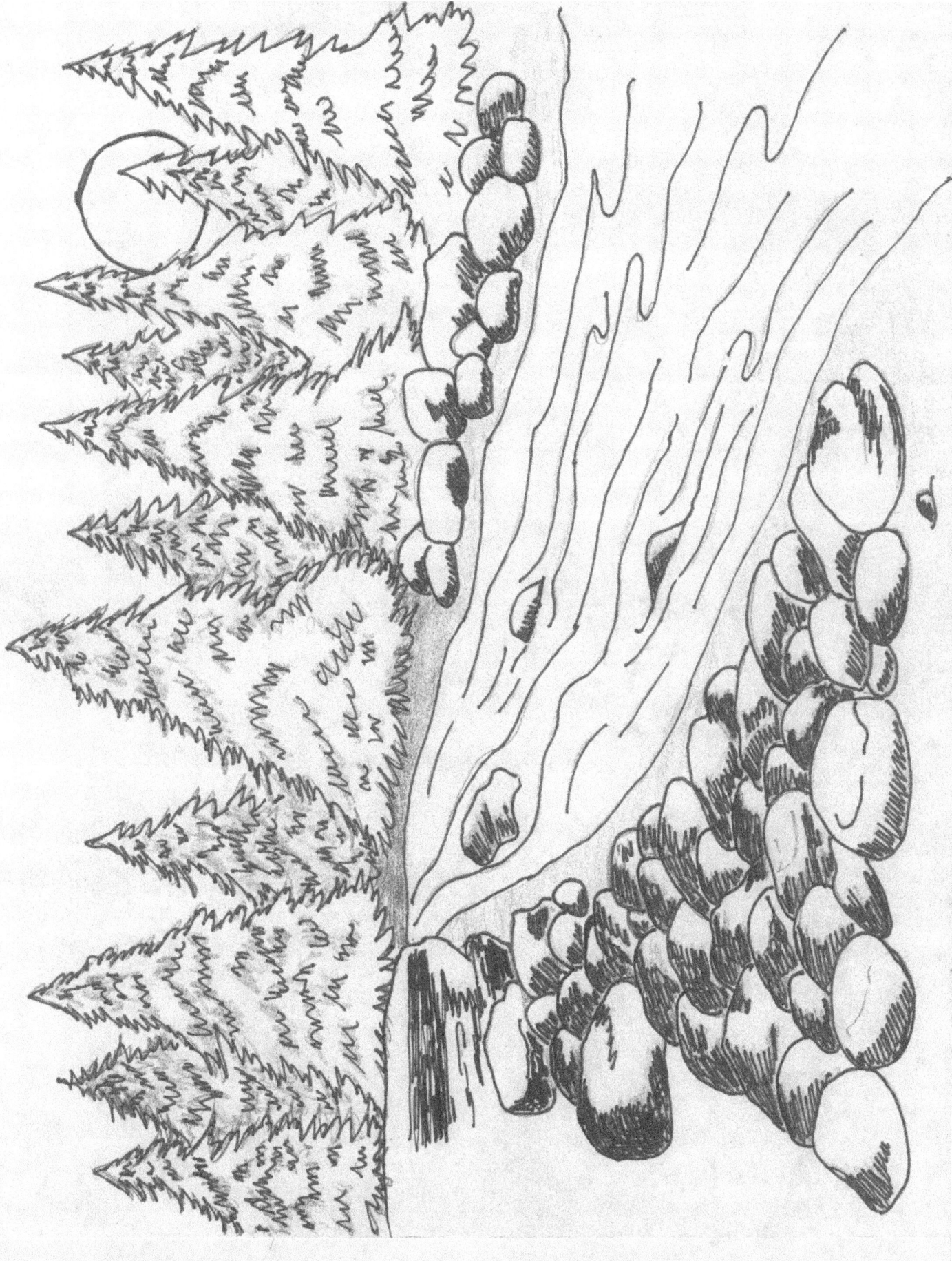

Introducing "The Art of Coloring " adult coloring books.

Adult coloring books are the same as children's coloring books except more detail.

I got started creating coloring books about a year ago. I have always carried my art work to appointments when I knew I was going to have a wait period. It helped me with anxiety and panic attaches. When I was asked why I brought my sketch book to the doctors office I just told them "That is my prozac."My doctors don't ask me how I am doing anymore , they ask me "What kind of artwork do we have today."

One day I received a promotional mail piece from a book company and one page was a coloring page with the phrase. Color your stress away. A light went on. I am an accomplished artist, Illustrator I can start my own line of adult coloring books.

I started talking to people about the coloring books and found out that a lot of people men and women likes to color. Coloring books are fast growing to a number one selling product in this country. People everywhere are coloring in adult coloring books.

Drawing pictures and coloring has helped me with my anxiety and panic attaches. It has mellowed me out and makes life a lot easier. It has been proven to help people with ADD, ADHD, and Bipolar disorder. It even helps some with Alzheimer. There are a lot of emotional benefit when someone take the time out of the busy day to color some pictures.

Coloring Books are helping People in every day life, Old Folks Homes , assisted living facilities and more. It seems to mellow them out and makes life easier for them. I have enclosed information about our books. 10% of our sales goes to sending books to nursing homes. If you are a customer and would like some books sent to your local nursing home. We will make arrangement to get them coloring books in your name.

Thank You for considering our Coloring books.

MJ. Short
Artist, Illustrator.
Publisher
(256) 201-7584

We Do custom coloring books for children's birthday parties, weddings, businesses or any other reason you may want a custom coloring books. Coloring Books are a great fund raiser.

How much fun is it when your child has a coloring book to give a personalized coloring book to his/her playmates at a birthday party or to give to guest at a wedding.

Great for advertising when promoting a business or Fund Raiser

There are a lot of reasons to order a customized coloring book. Minimum order is 20 books when ordering a customize book. Customized coloring books are $10.99 each, 30 pages, minimum order 20 books. You can order as many as you wish. You let us know what you would like to see what kind of pictures put into the book.

The book is for :_____

Personalized name you wish to be added to the book. Child's name, business name, couple's etc.

_____

What type of pictures would you like to see in the book? _____

_____

_____

_____

_____

_____

Name:_____

Address:_____

City:_____State:_____Zip:_____

Phone:_____

Number of books ordered._____

We include a starter set of pencils. $15.99 each. Two books $25.99 Three books $35.99

Purchase any two books and shipping is FREE

BB352017…..Butterflies and Blossoms_40 pages_____

FP352017…..Flower Power _ 30 pages_____

LS352017….Landscapes__30 pages _____

CS352017….Color Your Stress Away_30 pages_____

FP452017….Flower Patterns_40 pages_____

FPPV352017 …Flower Power pocket version._40 pages____

SM352017….Simple Mandals_40 pages _____

FT352017….Final Touch Outdoors ..50 pages_____

10% of all orders will be used to donate coloring books

to nursing homes. When you order please include the name

and address of the nursing home you wish books to go to.

The books will be sent in your name.

check the books you wish to order. If one book add $6.00 shipping and Handling. If you order 2 or more shipping is free. Starter box of colored pencils will be included.

Name:_____

Address:_____

_____

City:_____State:____Zip:_____

Phone:_____

Email:_____

Be sure to include the appropriate funds. Cash check or money order.

_____Yes,____No I would like to receive a complete catalog of coloring books and products